Managing the Design Process
Implementing Design

ROCKPORT

First published in the United States of America by
Rockport Publishers, a member of
Quayside Publishing Group
100 Cummings Center
Suite 406-L
Beverly, Massachusetts 01915-6101
Telephone: (978) 282-9590
Fax: (978) 283-2742
www.rockpub.com

Library of Congress Cataloging-in-Publication Data
Stone, Terry Lee.
  Managing the design process-implementing design : an
essential manual for the working designer / Terry Lee Stone.
       p. cm.
  Includes bibliographical references and index.
  ISBN-13: 978-1-59253-619-1
  ISBN-10: 1-59253-619-0
  1. Commercial art--Management. 2. Design services--
Management. I. Title. II. Title:
Essential manual for the working designer.
  NC1001.S77 2010
  741.6068--dc22

                                        2010018824
                                           CIP

ISBN-13: 978-1-59253-619-1
ISBN-10: 1-59253-619-0

10 9 8 7 6 5 4 3 2 1

Design: AdamsMorioka, Inc.

Printed in China

Managing the Design Process
Implementing Design

An Essential Manual for the Working Designer

Terry Lee Stone

BEVERLY MASSACHUSETTS

ROCKPORT PUBLISHERS

Contents

Introduction

Great graphic design doesn't happen by magic or in a vacuum. It is the result of intricately orchestrated collaboration between a designer and his or her client. It also requires well-managed collaboration within a design team composed of individuals with various skills and expertise. Although graphic design has great power to captivate, persuade, motivate, and delight, it would never get off the ground without effective planning, organization, and management. *Managing the Design Process—Implementing Design* is a guide to understanding and using best practices in design management that work to bring design concepts through to successful completion.

This book is about how to actualize design ideas and manage the collaborative process effectively. It may require learning some new language, tools, and techniques. In *Managing the Design Process—Concept Development*, the focus was on framing a design problem and developing design solutions that help to meet a client's business goals. This challenge requires acquiring useful input and research, analyzing and processing this information, and then developing innovative design concepts that mirror and advance the client's business strategy. In essence, this is design leadership—the process of utilizing design as a management tool to determine and achieve strategic goals.

Managing the Design Process—Implementing Design has a more tactical emphasis. It focuses on design management—coordinating and directing design resources to achieve a stated objective. Design management utilizes the people and procedures required to transform a design concept into a designed piece, be it a logo, brochure, or website. Design management activities take methodical planning and meticulous practice. Every graphic design project requires leadership and management at different stages of the design development cycle.

Digging deeper into design management, this book uncovers and explains the secrets of project management—the oversight of design jobs with specific deliverables, budgets, and schedules. Not taught in art school, good project management is the key to delivering design on time, on budget, and to the client's satisfaction. Project management is the key to profitability, which is essential to the health and wealth of any design practice. All of this must occur while maintaining creative excellence. It's a constant juggling act.

Design Collaboration

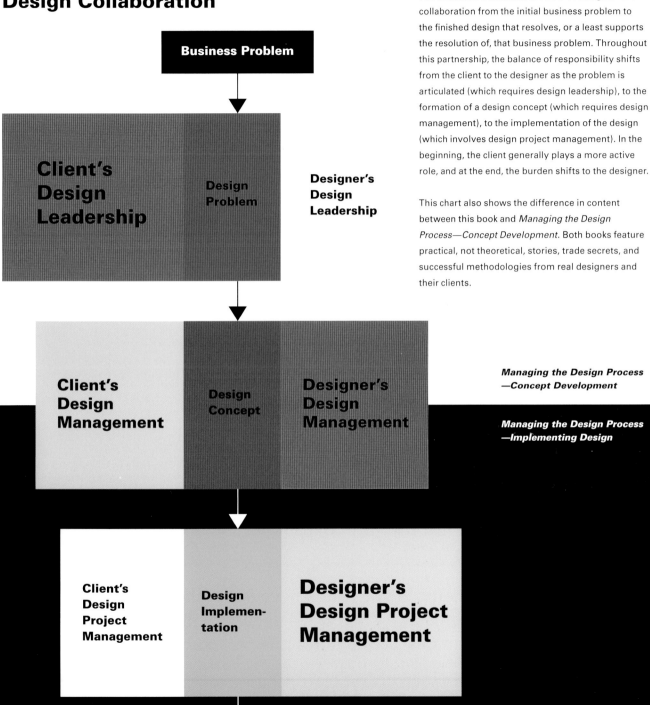

Business Problem

Client's Design Leadership

Design Problem

Designer's Design Leadership

Client's Design Management

Design Concept

Designer's Design Management

Client's Design Project Management

Design Implementation

Designer's Design Project Management

Finished Design

Managing the Design Process —Concept Development

Managing the Design Process —Implementing Design

The chart at left indicates the flow of designer–client collaboration from the initial business problem to the finished design that resolves, or a least supports the resolution of, that business problem. Throughout this partnership, the balance of responsibility shifts from the client to the designer as the problem is articulated (which requires design leadership), to the formation of a design concept (which requires design management), to the implementation of the design (which involves design project management). In the beginning, the client generally plays a more active role, and at the end, the burden shifts to the designer.

This chart also shows the difference in content between this book and *Managing the Design Process—Concept Development*. Both books feature practical, not theoretical, stories, trade secrets, and successful methodologies from real designers and their clients.

How to Use This Book

This book is a behind-the-scenes look at how designers actualize their design concepts to create finished pieces. The designers featured in this book share insights, ideas, and tactics from the real world of design management. More than discussing their aesthetic choices alone, these designers let us in on the practical aspects of their collaborations with clients and other creatives. Breaking down project management procedures, we can examine the processes required to produce great design on time and on budget in a way that makes both the client and the designer happy.

Here are some key things to take away from the case studies and project profiles in this book:

How do designers structure projects for maximum efficiency and quality? Would this work for your studio?

What type of agreements do designers and clients engage in? Do formal contracts work? How does your contract measure up?

How do designers manage a creative brief? Can you use any of these techniques?

What tools do designers use to manage their projects? Did software help? How hard is it to institute, and is it worth doing in your studio?

What issues or concerns did the client have about the design? How were these addressed? What kinds of communication were required for the client to accept the designer's recommendations?

How was profitability increased? Would you be better off making a different choice?

What is the finished design? What delivery medium was used? Was it effective? What do you think of it?

Managing the Design Process

In each client relationship, graphic designers follow the same systematic phases of work that allow them to consistently produce results. Different designers may have different terms for these steps, but all of them employ something similar. No matter what they call it, every phase of work in design must be managed well and consistently.

The following pages contain a design process chart illustrating systematic project work flow, from concept to completion. You can modify this model to suit any design project. It serves as an outline of the interactions between designer and client as work progresses.

Constraints That Affect the Design Process

The following constraints greatly affect the phases of work in the design process chart:

Communication:
Timely and effective communication and sharing knowledge throughout the process is necessary. Incomplete or lax communication will sabotage design.

Scope of Work:
Massive projects may require repetition of certain phases, while smaller projects with less complexity may combine steps.

Timing:
Compressed schedules mean shortened phases and skipped details. Luxurious time frames allow for more extensive work in each phase.

Budget:
Less money equals less work. Large budgets accommodate more work through more lengthy and involved procedures.

Delivery Media:
Choice of delivery medium can mean more (or less) extensive collaboration with other types of collaborators and can affect the process.

Design management means understanding and taking charge of the process by which design is created. Stack the deck for favorable outcomes by fully developing the possibilities inherent in each phase of work.

Design Process Overview Chart

Discover		Define	
①	**②**	**③**	**④**
Project Initiation	**Orientation/ Research**	**Strategy**	**Exploration**

• Client identifies need or goal
• Client develops preliminary budget
• Client develops preliminary schedule
• If possible, client creates preliminary creative brief
• Client identifies potential designers and contacts them
• Client and designer meet for preliminary discussion and portfolio review
• Client creates and sends out RFP (request for proposals)
• Designers respond and submit proposal for design services
• Client accepts proposal and confirms designer
• Designer typically requests deposit payment on the project
	• Client provides any relevant background information and materials
	• Designer leads client through creative briefing sessions
	• Client and designer commence research as needed regarding
	   Competitive landscape
	   Target audience
	   Market research
	   Design research
	Using any or all of the following:
	   Observation
	   Interviews
	   Questionnaires
	   Audits
	• Client and designer confirm any technical or functionality parameters
	• Client and designer confirm needs assessment and begin design problem formulation
		• Designer analyzes and synthesizes the research and information gathered
		• Designer develops design criteria
		• Designer develops functionality criteria
		• Designer develops media delivery method plan
		• Designer presents all of the above for client input or approval
		• Designer develops and articulates a strategy for the design
		• Designer develops preliminary plans: information architecture, pagination maps, and/or wireframes (if appropriate)
		• Designer presents all of the above for client input or approval
			• Based on client-approved strategy, designer develops preliminary design concepts
			• Designer's ideation can take the following forms:
			   Roughs/thumbnails/ sketches
			   Storyboards
			   Flowcharts
			   Mood/theme boards
			   Look and feel
			   POP (proof of principal) or proof of concept models
			• Designer presents the above to client for discussion, input, and approval
			• Client provides insights and initial validation that the concept direction will meet the project's stated goals and objectives
			• Typically, the designer will create several alternative concepts that will be narrowed down to only a couple of concept ideas to be developed further.

Goal of this phase:	**Goal of this phase:**	**Goal of this phase:**	**Goal of this phase:**
• Establish Basic Project Parameters • Selection of Designer	• Clarify Objectives and Goals • Identify Opportunities • Set Broad-based Requirements	• Develop overall Strategy • Determine design Approach • Confirm List of Deliverables	• Generate Preliminary Ideas • Evaluate these Ideas

◄────── Understand ──────►◄────── Ideate ────────

Develop

Deliver

5 | Development

6 | Refinement

7 | Production

8 | Manufacture/ Launch

9 | Project Completion

5 — Development

- Based on client-approved concept ideas, designer further develops the design concept(s).
- These further iterations of the concept(s) will be provided as tighter representations of the design:
  Comprehensive layouts
  Animatics
  Typical pages or spreads
  Preliminary Prototypes
- These will incorporate preliminary, often placeholder
  Copy/Messaging
  Imagery
  Motion
  Audio
- Designer presents the above to client for discussion, input, and approval
- Client provides insights and validation that the design direction will meet the project's stated goals and objectives
- Typically, the client will approve one design direction that will then be refined by the designer

6 — Refinement

- With a client-approved design direction, designer further refines the design.
- Typically, the changes/ modifications are
  Based specifically on client requests
  Minor in nature
  Finessing of aesthetic elements
- Designer presents the above to client for discussion, input, and approval
- Testing of the design may occur, and this may lead to another round of refinements. Testing may include
  Validation
  Usability testing
  Designer would then present these additional refinements to client for approval
- Designer initiates preproduction meeting with additional team members, if needed. These might include
  Printer/Fabricator
  Manufacturer
  Photographer/Illustrator
  Audio engineer
  Programmer

7 — Production

- With an approved design, the designer begins implementation of the design across all the required deliverables. This may include
  Print: *mechanicals/key lines, finished art, digital files, camera ready art, all elements final*
  Web: *modeling phase, detailed flowchart, all content, finished art for pages and graphic elements, programming, testing*
  Motion: *creating all project elements, animation making movies, shooting live action, editing, final rendering, mastering*
  Environment: *specifications, final prototyping, 3-D digital models, testing in preparation for production, coordinate/manage technical team*
  Packaging: *high-resolution file prep per specifications, color correction, structural prototyping*

8 — Manufacture/Launch

- Depending on the project and delivery media, the production materials are often handed over by the designer to others. Although other professionals outside the design firm actually do the work in most instances, the designer must supervise these suppliers and their work. This can include
  Prepress/Separator/ Printer
  Fabricator/Manufacturer
  Engineer/Programmer
  Media outlet
  Broadcast/on-air
  Launched on Web/live
- Designer may be engaged in the supervision or management of any or all of the above suppliers or it may be the client's responsibility
- Ongoing maintenance, especially in the case of Web design, may be an aspect of the project, or it will be determined under a separate agreement

9 — Project Completion

- Designer and client have a project debriefing (exit interview) to review
  Project procedures
  Outcomes: success or failure
  Feedback loops
  Additional opportunities
- Designer archives project files. Also, writes up a case study while the project details are fresh. This is preparation for the project as a self-promotional tool.
- Designer closes out and invoices project
- Client pays designer

Goal of this phase:
- Further Develop Ideas
- Select a Design Direction

Goal of this phase:
- Final Design Approved

Goal of this phase:
- Final Production
- Materials for Release

Goal of this phase:
- Design Materials
- Completed and in Use

Goal of this phase:
- Relationship building
- Sales opportunity for designer
- Begin new project

◄► ———— Execute ————►

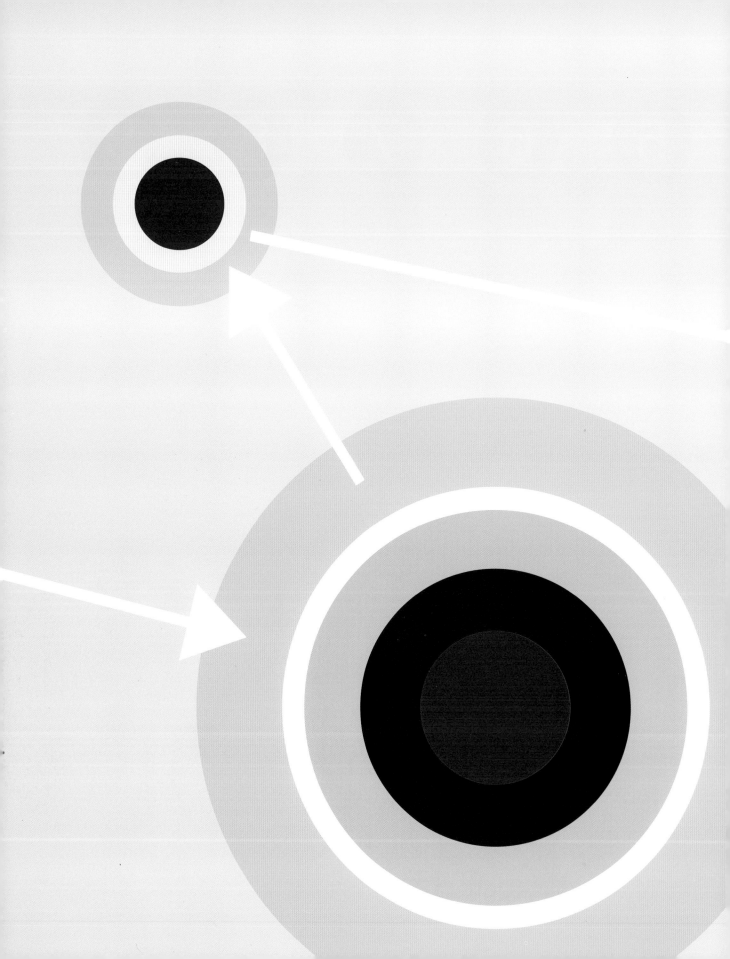

Chapter 1
Project Management

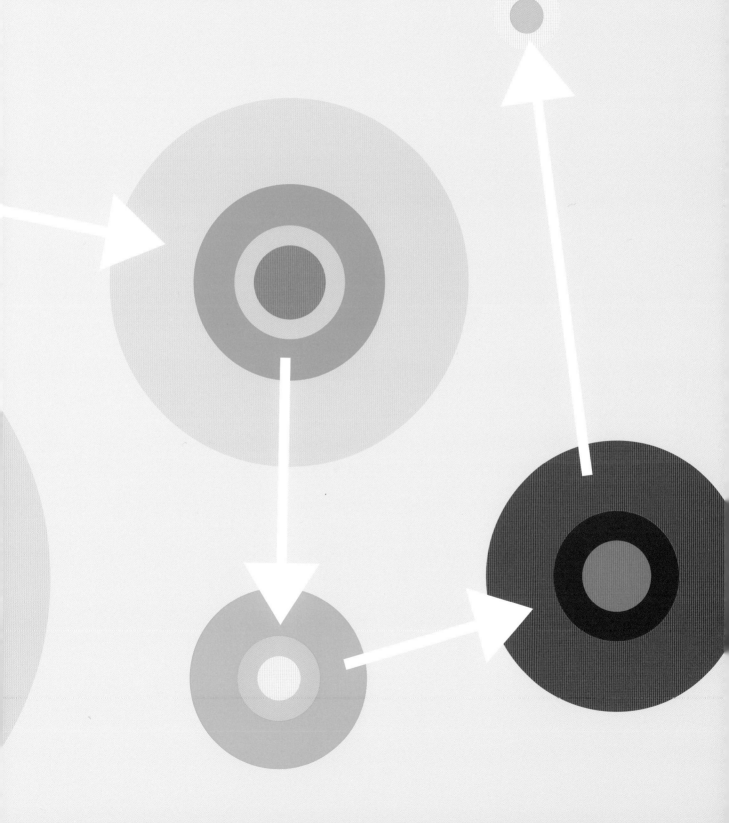

What Is Project Management?

A designer can have a great project, for the most amazing client, with a generous budget, and still barely break even. Designers can actually lose money, plus be tearing their hair out in frustration throughout the project because their team is disorganized, or worse, their client is out of control. Their project mismanagement can turn a great opportunity into a nightmare.

Good project management affects

- Creativity
- Quality
- Relationships
- Work flow
- Timelines
- Costs (fees and expenses)
- Profitability

In short, project management affects everyone on a design project. Managing a project consistently and well is critical to the project and to the designer's bottom line. In the short term, it makes projects more pleasurable and profitable. In the long term, good project management means a robust and rewarding design practice. It's worth the time and effort to understand project management best practices, use tried-and-true tools, and fully implement some sort of project management program. It will pay for itself in financial terms and in client and design team satisfaction.

A Brief History

Project management has its origins in the multitasking, multiperson, highly schedule-driven construction industry. Early project management theory and practice came out of the building and manufacturing industries until the 1950s when corporations such as DuPont and Lockheed lead the way. In 1969, the Project Management Institute (PMI) was formed. By the 1970s, project management tools and techniques were primarily influenced by the nascent software industry. In 1981, PMI published *A Guide to the Project Management Body of Knowledge*, often referred to as the *PMBOK Guide*, which is essentially the bible of project management. Many believe we are stepping into a new era, with design and design process influencing professional project management theory.

In moving from bricks and mortar to bits and bytes, project management has landed more squarely in the realm of the designer. But should you run out and buy the *PMBOK Guide* to better run your design practice? Probably not. PMI espouses lots of procedures and methods that require so much work that the return on time invested would be very little for most designers. Instead, we should look to the project management procedures that graphic and industrial designers already use, sharpen them with some of the professional project management industry's methods, and develop our own theories and practices for graphic design project management.

The Constraints That Affect Projects

Traditionally, project management deals primarily with managing three constraints: cost, time, and scope. This is often visualized as a triangle, with some people placing quality at the center of the triangle as a unifying theme that informs the three constraints (see charts at upper right). However, because commercial projects must be delivered on time and within an agreed-upon cost and scope of work, as well as meet the client's and the designer's quality expectations, some people illustrate the constraint concept as a diamond, with quality as one of the four points (see charts at right). Regardless of the illustration you use, cost, time, scope, and quality are major mitigating factors that influence and impact all work.

RIGHT
Taking this idea a step further, design project management constraints can be diagrammed as a complex triangle that defines in more detail the terms time, cost, and scope.

Constraints

Tradition Project Management Triangle

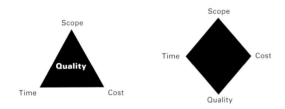

Variations on Tradition Project Management Triangle

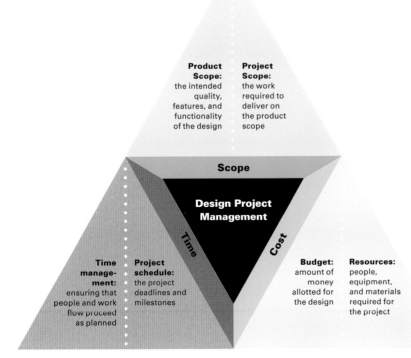

Detailed Design Project Management Triangle

Project Management Constraints

Time management is critical. Good time management means working within specific periods for each task and meeting incremental milestones such as presentations and other deadlines within a project schedule.

Cost management includes the overall budget the client has agreed to for design services and outside costs such as printing. Plus designers must marshal their resources appropriately, ensuring that the right people, equipment, and materials are employed to complete the design.

Scope is a bit more complex conceptually, but designers must be mindful of two aspects: the product scope, or the overall quality of the design they are delivering, which should be summarized in the creative brief (see page 31); and the project scope, or the work, measured in specific tasks per phase, that is required to deliver the expected product scope. Designers must always be aware of these issues to keep the project in balance and moving forward.

Design Means Constraints

Each assignment requires a unique, short-term management structure comprised of the designer, the client, and their respective teams who work together during the project. Although designers can affect constraint parameters, most designers can't control them, and instead work within the parameters the client has set; time constraints, budgets, and at least some of the people required for the project are frequently dictated by the client. Combine that with communication goals, audience needs, and brand infrastructure, which also all affect design, and that's a lot to manage.

Overview of Project Management

Estimates are never perfect, and creativity is hard to schedule so that it fits into neat little time units. But in business, time equals money. Designers must deliver their creativity in a timely fashion so that they can move on to the next client opportunity. If they don't, they may end up working at below minimum wage, or even lose money, in spite of decent client budgets and plenty of projects lined up. Without good management, a designer's business will fail.

What's the best way to tackle design project management? This book will break down some best practices in detail. These nitty-gritty details of running a business are boring compared to the exciting intellectual and creative challenges that are at the heart of design work. Unfortunately, creative activities typically comprise less than half the time spent on a design project; usually, most time is spent on technical, communication, management, clerical, and billing issues, all in service to the project. The reality is, these activities can make or break a design project and a design firm.

The process work flowchart on pages 10–11 breaks down the phases of work on a typical design project, including the tasks typically completed in the phase. Each task affects the project's schedule, costs, and scope. Therefore, each task must be defined, resourced, scheduled, and managed.

Common Mistakes in Project Management

Project management can be sabotaged in millions of ways. Here are some of the most common mistakes graphic designers make:

1. Lack of Commitment:
This often occurs because so many firm owners are creative directors. They want to commit to project management, but it cramps their style.

2. Lack of Clarity:
This is usually the result of poorly defined goals and objectives. This causes confusion, lack of clear-cut action, or even mistakes.

3. Poor Communication:
This stems from not obtaining or disseminating information in a timely fashion to the design team and/or the client.

4. Wrong Person:
The project manager doesn't possess the skills or temperament for the job. So, even if the owner is on board with the concept of project management, he or she has sabotaged the activity by hiring the wrong person to implement it.

5. Disorganization:
Project management is about determining the components of the design project, and that means keeping a lot of details in order. Whether it is personal or companywide, disorganization is fatal to project management.

Design Project Management Cycle

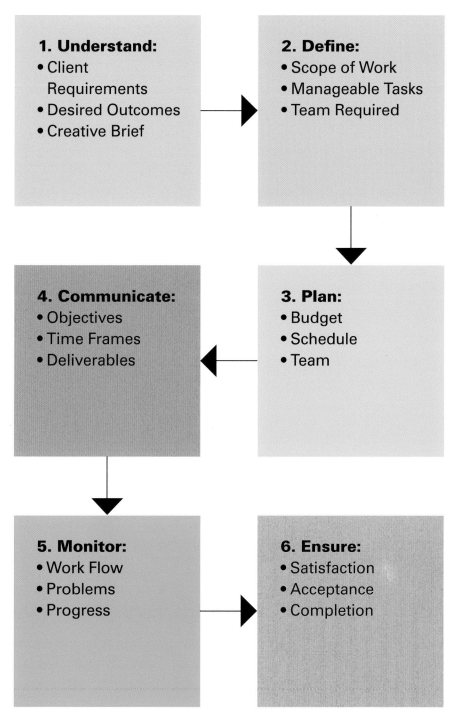

1. Understand:
- Client Requirements
- Desired Outcomes
- Creative Brief

2. Define:
- Scope of Work
- Manageable Tasks
- Team Required

4. Communicate:
- Objectives
- Time Frames
- Deliverables

3. Plan:
- Budget
- Schedule
- Team

5. Monitor:
- Work Flow
- Problems
- Progress

6. Ensure:
- Satisfaction
- Acceptance
- Completion

This diagram describes the steps in the design project management process. Whether it is a large or small assignment, someone must manage each aspect from start to finish.

Project Profile in Project Management
Frolick designed by Asylum / Singapore

Frolick Frozen Yogurt Bar brings the frozen yogurt craze to Singapore. Asylum, a design studio that also operates a retail store, a workshop, and a record label, gave the Frolick brand a politically incorrect attitude. The store frontage is dotted with badges sporting catchy slogans such as "We stay hard longer," "Size does matter," and "I like it topless." These slogans appear as button graphics on everything from serving cups to store interiors. They're also on buttons that are given as collectibles to fans and customers, who look forward to updated buttons with each new store opening. "We wanted to approach yogurt in a fun, unexpected way," says Asylum creative director Chris Lee. "The pull factor is tasty yogurt, good design, and a spunky attitude."

BELOW
Frolick is frosty, preservative-free frozen yogurt that's low in fat and sugar but high in flavor. The graphics (below, left) express a fun yet cheeky attitude, appealing to a quirkier, unconventional customer than most yogurt brands target, as seen in a series of promotional buttons, (lower left), which also appear on the serving container (below, right).

OPPOSITE
Rolling out a full branding program takes coordination. All the graphics—from environments to gift cards (opposite, above) to promotional booklets such as the Frolick Invaluable Tips on Courtship and Dating and Breakups (opposite, below)—had to be in place the day the first Frolick store opened. The Asylum designers created the identity system and the companion website for their client.

According to creative director
Chris Lee, here is how work flows
though Asylum:

1. Brief is handed to designers
2. Designers start research
3. Designers work on individual
   concepts
4. 10 groups of 3 will meet
   and brainstorm
5. First internal review
6. Ideas are short-listed and refined
7. Second internal review
8. Boss will inject a last-minute idea
   that he saw from a magazine
9. Designers will execute that
   idea unwillingly
10. Client is presented with the idea

	Cup A	Cup B +1 Topping	Cup C +2 Toppings		Cup A	Cup B +1 Topping	Cup C +2 Toppings	Assorted Toppings
	$3.50	$4.80	$6.30		$3.90	$5.30	$6.90	
	Original Frozen Yogurt				Flavoured Frozen Yogurt			$1.00 per serving

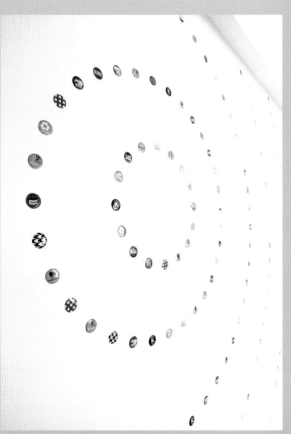

Cross Disciplinary, Cross Cultural

Asylum is an idea company founded by designer Chris Lee. Since its inception in 1999, the firm has excelled in cross-disciplinary projects that include interactive design, product development, environmental and interior design, packaging, branding, and graphic design. "We draw our inspirations from fashion, design, architecture, culture, flower arrangement, and *tai chi*," says Lee. Their perspective is both local and global. "Singapore creativity is increasingly being sought after internationally, as our sensibility and design are highly exportable," Lee explains. "Coming from a multicultural environment, our work touches upon certain basic human emotions that can communicate across cultures." Frolick is one of Asylum's best examples of cross-disciplinary skills.

OPPOSITE AND THIS PAGE
One thing that makes Asylum Singapore unique as a creative consultancy is that it has its own retail store, The Asylum. Their store sells everything from limited-edition sneakers, quirky toys, and handmade designer crafts to international art magazines and music CDs from obscure, experimental indie bands. Having their own store provides creative director Chris Lee and his team with unique insight into retail design. Asylum utilized that knowledge for Frolick. The designers created fun, inviting super graphic wall panels and artwork incorporating the cheeky buttons in massive swirl patterns as seen in the photos.

Project Management Enhances Creativity

When designers attend art school, they focus on creativity and using graphic elements in new and interesting ways to communicate specific messages. Some designers acquire organizational skills by managing their school assignments in ways that help them work more efficiently. Others never learn.

Good work habits are essential for delivering a design that meets the client's expectations. Orchestrating all aspects of a project well creates a calm confidence that allows designers to do their best work.

Well-managed projects help designers to be more creative by enabling them to
- Establish better client relationships
- Ensure less confusion throughout the project
- Identify clear objectives and deliverables
- Provide more useful and strategic information
- Define blocks of time to do the work
- Assist in creating more enjoyable team interaction
- Provide the proper budget to accomplish goals
- Create an outlined and agreed-upon review process
- Articulate milestones
- Make better decisions
- Create a sense of shared and coordinated efforts with the client
- Boost respect by supporting the perception of professionalism
- Help mitigate problems while they are small

All of this results in better design by allowing designers to work under the best circumstances to produce their best ideas. It also creates an atmosphere of professional competence that positions designers as true professionals who clients count on time and time again.

Paprika Philosophy
Paprika—headed by cofounders Joanne Lefebvre and Louis Gagnon, along with creative director René Clément—has made its mark in Quebec and internationally. The visually stunning design is due in no small part to the trust and respect they have from their clients "We have a specific approach to what we do—not so much a style, but an approach," explains Clément. "We don't want to do what is expected. We like to break the mold." Paprika works with clients that are willing to take risks and go further. "That's what we're good at," Clément continues. "When clients are happy with that, we have an amazing relationship that lasts a very long time. We do research, of course, but the element we find most essential to our work is instinct. That instinct— the sense that 'it should feel like this'—usually ends up being the best approach for our clients."

Project Profile in Project Management:
Les Allusifs designed by Paprika / Montréal, Canada

Paprika has enjoyed a long-standing working relationship with the small publishing company, Les Allusifs. Paprika created the publisher's identity and branding, as well as many book covers over the years. The identity features a red circle containing the company name Les Allusifs (which translates to "the Allusives"), a reference to the intellectually and artistically challenging French-language book titles it publishes. As the collection appeals to a range of French-speaking cultures, the simplicity of Les Allusifs' identity system works as an elegantly simple unifying device. The logo and circle are stark red and black graphic elements that serve as unifying devices. "We created a strong unity, a 'family tie,' that holds them together."

"Les Allusifs' identity program has allowed them to distinguish themselves, while keeping an intellectual, artistic focus," says Paprika cofounder Louis Gagnon.

BELOW
The identity does not intrude. It unifies a collection of eclectic short novels in French from authors of various nationalities from this unique Canadian publishing house.

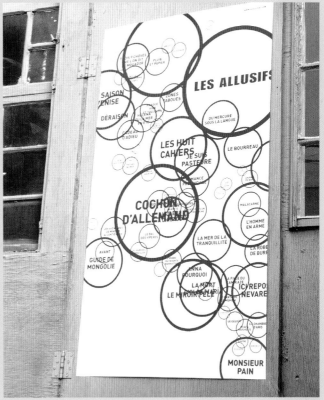

Traits for Success in Project Management

1 **Problem Solving:**
Be committed to finding solutions, regardless of how complex the situation seems. Don't procrastinate; start untangling the mess as soon as possible. Keep problems off the project manager's desk and with the design team, where something can be done to solve the problem and move the project forward.

2 **Negotiation:**
Often, problem solving means compromising, which means some negotiation must occur. Look for the most equitable solution. Be flexible. It's far better to move forward with a less-than-perfect plan than to not move at all.

3 **Urgency:**
Working in a timely fashion is expected in today's fast-paced business environment. This means you must employ a sense of urgency in all project management activities. "Keep the ball rolling" is the mantra.

4 **Focus:**
Someone has to sweat all the details—from who should be included in the conference call, to what the correct disclaimer copy is, to where the invoice should be mailed. Focusing on the minutia makes the project flow.

Agility:
Thinking creatively on your feet and quickly reacting in a professional manner while sidestepping personality clashes are exercises in flexibility. Doing this with speed and grace equals agility. This behavior will serve the project well.

Decisiveness:
Leadership and management require ongoing decision making. The inability to make correct choices for the team and the project will stymie a job.

Risk Taking:
At some point in every project, designers will have to act boldly and take a risk. Maybe all the information hasn't gelled or a leap of faith in the schedule needs to occur—whatever it is, it may require guts but not foolishness.

Balance:
All projects face constraints—most often related to time, cost, and scope. Project management means continually juggling and balancing these factors.

Project Profile in Project Management:

Illumivision designed by smashLAB / Vancouver, BC, Canada

Illumivision

SmashLAB is an interactive design studio led by partners Eric Shelkie and Eric Karjaluoto. SmashLAB works with its clients to position organizations and develop marketing strategies through the use of technology. This was the case with Illumivision, which designs and manufactures high-powered LED fixtures for architectural lighting and commercial applications. The client's previous collateral and website were confusing, were costly to create and distribute, and lacked a distinctive personality.

SmashLAB completed its work in three stages. First, the designers created and launched the initial website, which took ten weeks. Thanks to that project's success, the designers were brought back to create new print materials, which took six weeks. Later, smashLAB aligned the Illumivision brand identity over eight weeks. This phased development required consistent project management to work efficiently over time. Karjaluoto says, "Normally, we start with brand development and craft a website, but an identity was established that dovetailed nicely with the online property."

High contrast and cinematic, dark back-grounds are brought to life by a broad spec-trum of lighting, capturing visitors' attention on this website. The overall design system works in a variety of online and print mat-erials, blending a luscious visual aesthetic with a certain technical balance that mirrors Illumivision's products and has resulted in a 225 percent increase in international inquiries and sales since the design was launched.

BELOW
"Prior to our involvement, Illumivision concentrated primarily on hard goods they created, instead of the visual impact their products have," explains smashLAB creative director Eric Karjaluoto. "As such, we worked to highlight these char-acteristics as they are seductive." In this way, the theme of "illumina-tion" informed all of smashLAB's design decisions.

OPPOSITE
The target audience for the Illumivision website consists primarily of architects and lighting designers, followed by engineers and specifiers, and finally, endusers. Messaging identified the advan-tages of illumination products, while small photos lend impact and focus the visitor on product benefits.

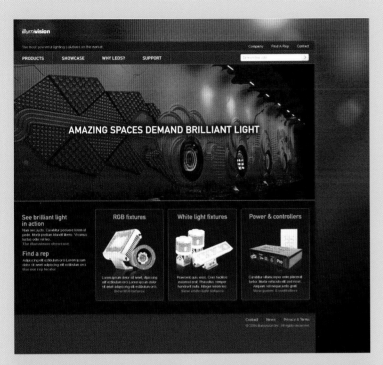

Keep It Simple:

Eric Karjaluoto reveals
the realities of project
management at smashLAB:

**Q. Do you have a project management
philosophy?**

A. If we do, it's not something we researched
and implemented. Our process has evolved
out of necessity. Ultimately, we're mindful
that almost every aspect of our work is better
when we employ a systemized procedure.
Establishing those methods has been a matter
of trial and error, and we've consistently honed
our approach over the years.

Q. Do you have any tips for success?

A. When we started the company, we wanted
to lock down as many elements of our process
as possible and be aware of every small step
of the project. This turned out to be overly
restrictive and time consuming. Suddenly,
we were spending our days updating Gantt
charts and obsessing over details that were
really critical.

While it was useful to break down steps and
monitor progress, we found that it's better
to look at some of this as a guide rail: helpful
for structure, but not the gospel. Meanwhile,
you have to find what works best for your
particular organization. Some of our best
project management tools are simple task lists
and Post-it notes. That wouldn't work in an
organization of 500 people, but at our size,
it's pretty sticky.

Chapter 2
Project Setup

Getting Design Off to a Good Start

All design engagements generally follow this encapsulation of the designer's work flow:

- Listen to a problem.
- Think about it.
- Form ideas.
- Sketch some design solutions.
- Present/sell the design.
- Get it approved.
- Make finished artwork.
- Possibly hand it off to others to produce.
- Deliver it.
- Bill it.

Although their projects may vary in complexity and duration, designers perform these activities over and over throughout their careers.

Organizing and Persuading

Effective use of organization and persuasion skills determines whether a design project succeeds or fails. In design and project management, to organize means to create a workable structure and prepare for the design team's activities. It means taking responsibility for the orderly progression of the work required.

In project management, persuasion concerns the designer's ability to cause someone—whether it is the client or members of the design team—to do something required during the project. Setting the stage for empowerment and having the stakeholders in a design project agree upfront to be managed is critical. In this way, persuasion begins the moment the designer takes on a project.

Basic and Broad Strokes First

Laying a good foundation is an important first step for any design project, large or small. Start by answering these simple questions that lead to forming a creative brief:

- Who is the client? What is their problem/need?
- What are we doing for them? What is our known list of deliverables?
- When is it due? What are the project milestone dates?
- Who do we want to work with on this job (internal /external team members)?
- What is our budget? How will we allocate it?

The importance of obtaining this information and summarizing it in a creative brief cannot be stressed enough. You should write a creative brief at the beginning of each project. The creative brief allows design concept work to be initiated, and continues to guide project management during design implementation.

Components of a Creative Brief

Components of a Creative Brief

1. Background Summary:
Who is the client? What is the product or service? What are the strengths and weaknesses? Ask the client for any documents (research, reports, etc.) that help to understand the situation.

2. Overview:
What is the project? What are we designing and why? Why does the client think they need this project? What opportunity will the design support?

3. Drivers:
What is our goal for this project? What is the purpose of our work? What are our top three objectives?

4. Audience:
Who are we talking to? What do they think of the client's product/service? Why should they care?

5. Competitors:
Who is the competition? What are they telling the audience that we should be also telling them? What differentiates our client from their competitors?

6. Tone:
How should we be communicating? What adjectives describe the feeling or approach?

7. Message:
What are we saying with this piece exactly? Are the words already developed or do we need to write them? What do we want audiences to take away? Are there any disclaimers or legal information that must be included?

8. Visuals:
How should these images look? Are we developing new images or picking up existing ones? If we are photographing them, who, what, and where are we shooting, and why? Are we commissioning illustrations or picking up stock?

9. Details:
What is the list of deliverables? What is the delivery medium? Are there any preconceived ideas, format parameters, or limitations and restrictions regarding the design? What are the timeline, schedule, and budget?

10. People:
Who are we reporting to? Who exactly is approving this work? Who needs to be informed of our progress and by what means?

Contracts Assist Project Management

The creative brief is just one of the tools that guides designers in their work. Another vital document is the contractual agreement between the designer and the client. This agreement—sometimes called a proposal, estimate, or deal memo—is a formal contract for design services to be rendered to a client for a set fee.

Never Practice Design without a Contract

No designer should begin work on a project without a legally binding agreement. Why? Because it is one of the most important tools for

- Establishing the professional nature of the design engagement
- Defining the work to be done, including the number of revisions
- Outlining the process by which the work will be accomplished
- Formalizing the working relationship between the designer and client
- Building trust and, ultimately, acceptance of the designer's work
- Acting as a powerful communication vehicle for both designer and client to visualize how work will progress
- Ensuring that the designer is not taken advantage of and the client gets what they expect
- Providing a substantiating document that will stand up in court or in legal arbitration if the designer–client relationship turns bad

Although a well-written and signed designer–client agreement can stand up in a court of law, nine times out of ten, the most important role of the designer–client agreement is as a communication tool. It is a means for the designer and the client to discuss and define the scope of work the designer will provide, and the compensation the designer will receive, for a project they are about to work on together. Once agreed to, it becomes an excellent reference point to guide all design work and project management thereof.

Designer–Client Agreements

A detailed discussion of all the variations and permutations a graphic designer's contractual agreements could assume is beyond the scope of this book. For our purposes, it's important to understand that you need to create a formal written agreement for every client project you take on. To be effective, the agreement should include the following:

▶ **Basic contact information:**
The name, company name, address, phone number, and email address of the designer and the client should appear on the document.

▶ **The date:**
The document must be dated as a reference point. This will also help avoid confusion if subsequent amended versions of the agreement are created.

▶ **Basic project information:**
Use the project name the client uses. Provide a brief project outline, sometimes called the scope of work or statement of work (SOW). Describe the work to be done, including any known deliverables, and summarize the project objectives. The summary should be specific enough to act as a starting point for the pricing of the project and initial design development phases.

▶ **Process outline:**
Indicate the iterative process—typically a sequence of steps or phases—that you recommend for the project. It is helpful to include the deliverables and milestones in each phase as a point of reference, and to check them off once they are completed. Also include the number of rounds/scope of revisions or refinements in each phase. Explain how the client will be integrated into the process and the client's responsibilities in each phase.

- ▶ **Fees and estimated expenses:**
  Fees are the designer's compensation for the work provided, and expenses are the out-of-pocket costs for materials, supplies, and any subcontractor work purchased specifically for the project.

- ▶ **Terms and conditions:**
  This is the legal language explaining your working relationship with the client. A series of clauses describes things such as payment terms, intellectual property rights transfer, promises about originality, a dispute resolution process, and other key information. Designers often start their careers with very simple terms and conditions, utilizing only a few clauses in their contracts. However, as they encounter problems in their client projects over the years, they tend to add additional language to deal with these unfortunate circumstances. Why not protect yourself well and use extensive terms and conditions language?

- ▶ **Dated signatures:**
  In many ways, this is the most important item in the agreement, because it shows that on a certain day a certain person representing the client agreed to the contents of the contract. A signed contract is hardcore proof of a deal.

Case Study Project Setup:

COLLINS: / BIG, Ogilvy & Mather / New York, New York USA

COLLINS:, led by Brian Collins, creates experiences, products, and digital interactions that transform and strengthen the relationship between organizations, brands, and people. "We use storytelling at every step of our approach: to understand the life of organizations, to articulate new possibilities, and to build ideas into experiences," says Collins. "Stories embrace a world of information and give it meaning. In doing so, they kick-start what a thousand bullet points cannot: action."

Helios

The agency's work, in conjunction with Boston-based architectural firm Office dA and BIG/Ogilvy, on the BP Helios House began with the concept of turning the typical gas station into a laboratory for sustainable design thinking. People stop for gas only because they have to. The design team's mission was to completely reinvent this U.S. service station experience. The result is a

solar-powered gas station that minimizes energy and water use, reducing costs and CO_2 emissions. Within weeks, Helios House became a new California landmark. It won the Leadership in Energy and Environmental Design (LEED) Certification, the nationally accepted benchmark for the construction and operation of high-performance green buildings.

OPPOSITE AND BELOW LEFT
The soaring canopy with its thousands of triangles was inspired by the BP Helios logo (which was previously designed by Landor) and by California roadside architecture. Its skin is embedded with ninety solar panels that produce 15,000 kWh of electricity to power the station, cut costs, and reduce annual CO_2 emissions by 2.5 tons (2.27 metric tons). For thousands of drivers, Helios House is a bright spot on their journey and inspiring proof of innovation from a company that seeks to go "Beyond Petroleum" (BP's tagline).

BELOW RIGHT
Pumps dispense not only gas, but also videos of energy-saving tips. The pumps were completely redesigned for ease of use. The COLLINS: team also designed training materials for station attendants to improve the customer experience and spark dialogue about energy efficiency. A website extends the conversation.

OPPOSITE
The corner of Olympic and Robertson boulevards in Los Angeles is the site BP chose for a new kind of gas station. The team developed unique green technologies and new customer experiences that are being tested for use in BP outlets in other locations. The transformation began behind construction screens, seen left, that featured an evolving supergraphic image. As the construction of the new station grew, so did the "grass" on the screens and the billboard at the site, turning the daily drive-by experience into anticipation. Six months later, the grass had grown to cover the billboards.

Case Study Project Setup:

COLLINS: / BIG, Ogilvy & Mather / New York, New York USA

BELOW

This is detail of the map given to visitors who want more information about the ideas behind Helios House. The map highlights each sustainability protocol at the station. Other printed collateral, such as postcards of the station, are wildly popular. The cards, which offer a curriculum of energy-saving ideas, are made of recycled paper and embedded with flower seeds so that people can plant them when they get home.

BELOW

Recycling is evident everywhere. The architects invented a better system that collects rainwater to irrigate the plants around the station. The restrooms are covered with a green roof of living plants, which reduces the need for heating and cooling. Floor-to-ceiling tiles in the restrooms are recycled glass in graphic mosaics. Lights, water, hand dryers, and even customizable music are activated by motion sensors to minimize the need for touching surfaces. ABC News reported drivers going miles out of their way just to use the restrooms at Helios House.

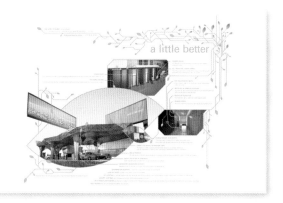

Metropolis

COLLINS: created the May 2009 cover of *Metropolis* magazine as a conceptual illustration of its Next Generation project, which celebrates innovation in renewable wind power. Brian Collins and his talented team—John Fullbrook III, Timothy Goodman, and Jason Nuttal—developed several smart directions, but the pinwheel/pylon juxtaposition piqued *Metropolis* editors' interest. The final cover—fun, bold, and hopeful—clearly reflects the idea of alternative energy sources.

BELOW

This issue of *Metropolis* features a story on wind power and how three designers have developed a way to achieve energy independence using the towers already in existence. In addition to the cover, COLLINS: designed a pinwheel on the inside pages that readers can cut out.

BELOW RIGHT

COLLINS: also developed an exhibit about the Next Generation project for *Metropolis* in which viewers are encouraged to write down and share their hopes for the future.

Case Study Project Setup:

COLLINS: / BIG, Ogilvy & Mather / New York, New York USA

Alliance for Client Protection

In conjunction with the Martin Agency, COLLINS: worked to tell the story of the urgent need for strong debate and forward-moving grassroots action on the issue of climate change. Its client, the Alliance for Climate Protection, is a nonprofit organization created by Nobel Peace Prize winner and former U.S. Vice President Al Gore. The organization's core message is "We can solve the climate crisis," and

it works to bring public attention to the issue. COLLINS: developed a strategy to transform parochial concerns into a social movement. The inspiration behind the branding is "We the People..." which are the opening words of the U.S. Constitution (the supreme law of the country). Within months, hundreds of thousands of people called for the global treaty and thousands more wrote the U.S. State Department. Two million people have since joined the effort.

BELOW LEFT
The story of a global problem transforming into a personal solution is captured in the logo. "We are the solution, but *we* still includes *me*," creative director Brian Collins explains. "We needed a unique visual language with clarity and warmth. So, we created a new typeface to do that. The letterforms are strongly declarative, while their rounded shapes convey a sense of openness and optimism."

You can't solve the climate crisis alone. But if we all work together, we can.

Join today.

wecansolveit.org

You can't solve the climate crisis

It's too big for one person to solve. It's going to take all of us, working together. The good news is, the solutions already exist. But the only way we're going to get them is by sending a powerful message to our corporations and our government. More than a million people, from all walks of life and across the political spectrum, have already come together to make their voices heard. Now we need you. Take one minute to join us at wecansolveit.org. **Because you can't solve the climate crisis on your own.**

But together we can.

The transformative logo is a key graphic unifying device. Ads, such as the newspaper spread below, aimed to enlist everyone as climate activists. The Alliance for Climate Protection sought to catalyze a cultural shift from a hyperindividualized society toward a shared future. Personal gear created by COLLINS: helped individuals identify themselves as members of a social movement, while helping to fund the organization.

The website is idea driven. The simple interface and no-nonsense design convey the sense of a citizen organization with a job to do. Design thinking alone ignited media coverage, a force-multiplier for budgets better invested in programs. COLLINS: helped the client put their effort where it has had the greatest tangible effect.

we | why join we | take action | about us | press & bloggers

we are millions of people speaking up for solutions. we can solve the climate crisis if we take action now. click here to join we today.

Action Alert: Join Al Gore in Davos by signing the climate petition.

Learn More >>

why join we

No single person will stop global warming, but by working together, we can make it a priority for government and business. We'll succeed because when people unite and call for action, change is inevitable. Together we can solve the climate crisis. more >>

VIEW ALL SOLUTIONS >>

about us

The We Campaign is a project of The Alliance for Climate Protection – a nonprofit, nonpartisan effort founded by Nobel laureate former Vice President Al Gore. Our ultimate aim is to halt global warming. more >>

RSS FEED >>

action alerts

◇ Support incentives for clean energy jobs more >>

◇ Sign the petition for a global treaty on climate change more >>

◇ Tell your friends about our first video more >>

VIEW ALL ACTIONS >>

Home >> Privacy & Legal >> FAQs >> Contact Us

search wecansolveit.org

Scoping the Work

To price any design project, designers must know what they're going to do for the client. That's simple enough. Just get a list of deliverables—the scope of work (SOW)—from the client and estimate the work based on the list. The only problem is that these lists are often preliminary, and don't end up being executed as initially outlined. Clients focus on the artifacts that designers create as though that was all their working relationship consisted of, and do not factor in the need for broad-based creative consultation. Designers regularly need to immerse themselves in research, analysis, and strategy before they can create anything. Plus, in these early discovery and strategic thinking phases, both business and creative insights are acquired that greatly impact and often alter the list of deliverables the designer will create.

Therefore, until this early design thinking is completed, an accurate SOW is illusive. It seems like a classic catch-22: designers can't estimate their fees until they understand what they're doing, but they can't know what they'll be doing until they begin the work. They don't want to start work until they have an agreed-upon fee. So, what is a designer to do?

Work-around for a Missing SOW

Here are a couple of scenarios to consider that can help jumpstart a project:

- Provide the client with an estimate for the discovery and strategy phases, with the caveat that subsequent work will be outlined and estimated upon completed and approved results of these phases.
- Submit an estimate/agreement based on the deliverables/SOW provided by the client. Add a change order caveat that lets the client know that any changes to the described SOW will result in a change order or amendment to the original estimate. (See more about change orders below.)

The bottom line is that you have to start someplace. With experience comes a better understanding of how a client's project will likely proceed. If you don't commit to something and can't hammer out an agreement, you have no project to go forward with. Defining the scope of work is tricky until there is an approved design strategy. Don't let this stop you. This is why pricing is about trying to assess the value of the work to the client's business. It's not about how many hours it will take or what artifacts will be created. It's about leveraging design's power in a consulting relationship with the client.

Change Orders

A change order is an amendment or addition to an existing approved and signed designer–client agreement. It means something has been added to—or changed within—the client-approved SOW, the process by which the work will be done, and/or the compensation to the designer.

In essence, a change order is a contract update that results in

- Additional fees and/or expenses to be paid by the client
- Additional time for the designer to complete the work

Rarely, a change order outlines a decrease in the designer's fees and/or expenses. Typically, designers opt to simply reduce the invoice amount to reflect the amended SOW rather than send a change order.

The change order document should look much like the original estimate or agreement. Legal terms and conditions can be omitted, and just referred to with language such as "Work covered under this change order is subject to the terms and conditions agreed to in the designer–client agreement dated x."

However, a change order should include

- Designer contact information
- Client contact information
- Date
- Name of project
- New scope of work
- New fees and expenses
- Dated signatures

Note in the original designer–client agreement that the designer may, if necessary, provide a change order. It helps keep clients in check because they understand their additional requests and changes will mean the designer expects additional time and money as a result.

Details Matter

Understanding that there are both perils and advantages in describing the SOW on a design project before a designer truly understands what needs to be done, what, then, is the best approach? Covering a few basic details will suffice.

Include the following when scoping:

- A brief summary of the project's goals and objectives.
- A list of the component deliverables—for example, an identity package comprising a logo, tagline, and basic business papers, including letterhead, envelope, and business card.
- In some cases, a simple definition of the component deliverables' structure or size—for example, the number of pages in a brochure or on a website. Often, until the design concept is developed, the precise structure is unknown.
- Delivery media. For example, is it an online project? Will the designer post it or simply provide files? For a print project, will the designer buy printing or hand off artwork to the supplier?
- Glaringly obvious services that are not included in the agreement. If such things as photography, copywriting, or manufacturing are relevant to the project, they should be included. These and other expense items might be purchased by the client, or perhaps the designer will estimate them later once the design concept is approved. Whatever the circumstance, make it clear.

Project Phase Descriptions

A further consideration in terms of scoping is to outline the design process. The chart on page 10–11 contains a thorough breakdown of the process most designers use. Using similar language in agreements and schedules aids the client in understanding design development as a professional, measurable activity. It takes the confusion out of the picture without diminishing or attempting to quantify the creative magic that nearly always occurs in any design project.

Here are some ways to describe the design work process:

- Outline all work in numbered phases and give each phase a descriptive title or name.
- List the major activities that will occur in each phase.
- List the deliverables for each phase.
- Specify the number of revisions a client may request in each phase. Try to define the complexity of these revisions; saying "one round of revisions" is broad, but it implies that the client must gather all changes at once and present them to the designer for inclusion at one time.
- Note the designer's expectations of the client in each phase. This informs the client that they must provide or approve something at a certain time before work can progress to the next phase.

Case Study in Organizing and Persuading:

Voice / Adelaide, Australia

Voice is a multidisciplinary design consultancy established in 1999 and led by codirectors Anthony De Leo and Scott Carslake. The firm delivers solutions in digital media, environmental, identity, packaging, promotional, publications, and typeface design. At the heart of the practice is a love of developing new ways of communicating with alluring and engaging visuals. Voice is also driven by a belief that the "unspoken voice often resonates the loudest," which can have some intriguing manifestations in terms of design. Both De Leo and Carslake are committed to a clear design process. "Discussing our process and how we develop, evaluate, and refine our work is very important to the client and their comfort levels with us," explains Carslake. "If they understand this, they have a better understanding and respect for our business. Then they know we don't just pull ideas from our back pockets."

Finsbury Green Report

Finsbury Green is Australia's leading commercial printer that operates under the world's best environmental practices and certifications. This international certification reassures customers that Finsbury Green's environment systems deliver genuine benefits, including the measuring and monitoring of all environmental impacts. For more than ten years, Finsbury has supplied printing services to Voice. "We have an excellent relationship with the managing director, one that has

turned into a great friendship," explains Carslake. In 2008, the printers commissioned Voice to create their sustainability report. Says Carslake, "The communication channels are very open. We openly discuss print margins, cost of stock, and so on, so when it came to this project, we dove straight in and didn't hold back on developing ideas that would get the attention of their audience, stakeholders, and staff."

BELOW AND OPPOSITE
Voice felt it could take Finsbury into a more powerful and dominating position in the "green" printing industry. Voice reinforced this message through the theme "You reap what you sow." Finsbury's workplace was turned into a natural wonderland with the staff photographed within the scenes going about their daily tasks, oblivious to the fanciful surroundings. Typography and graphs carried the nature theme throughout the document.

"If the client receives the right management and enjoys the experience along with the work, a strong, successful relationship will develop and we will be able to bring their brand to new places."
—Anthony De Leo, codirector, Voice

Case Study in Organizing and Persuading:

Voice / Adelaide, Australia

Polar

In 1977, Polar was founded to pioneer the development, manufacturing, and marketing of wireless heart rate monitors for sports professionals. Today, the company employs 1,200 people worldwide, has twenty-one subsidiaries globally, and manages a distribution network supplying more than 35,000 retail outlets in more

than eighty countries. Australian Polar distributor, Pursuit Performance, engaged Loud Communications to review sales and marketing activities, and provide a new brand and message for this leading global icon. Loud teamed with Voice to create a significantly different direction for the catalog, a major selling tool for the brand.

BELOW AND OPPOSITE
"Instead of simply redesigning the existing brochure and making it look and function better, we went back to the roots of their audience and products. This enabled us to create a new way of presenting the products and how they are sold to the market," says De Leo. "The client showed great courage in allowing us to take this path; we had to instill a lot of confidence and encourage them that this was a way to greater

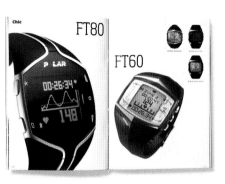

sales and brand presence," adds Carslake. The client was open to all manner of ideas but clearly focused on achieving greater sales outcomes. The resultant design expresses enthusiasm, energy, and a spirit of bravado that says, "We want to lead the world in how this product is marketed." The results speak for themselves: Launched in January 2009, the catalog had an immediate impact, with record sales achieved in only its first month.

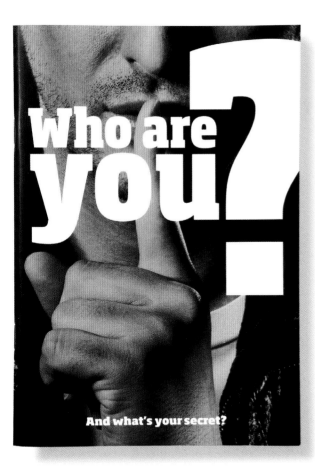

Management Process at Voice

Voice has worked with many different clients across several business sectors and feels that its clients are its partners in the design process. The lines of communication with clients are always open at Voice. Internally, the studio is set up in an open format specifically because communication is integral to the success of Voice's working environment.

The first key element of the process involves development of concepts and presentation of these concept(s) to the client for approval before production on the SOW commences. Clients must sign off on a concept before the job proceeds so that both Voice and the client monitor the quality of the idea.

One of Voice's codirectors will take that approved concept and either produce the entire SOW or work with the other codirector or designers. In this way, they are involved at every step. In addition, the studio's open environment allows other staff members to continue to overlook the process so that at all times, more than one person is watching the job develop and is monitoring the process so that it is being produced to the highest possible standard.

Finished art is prepared and a full working proof is supplied for the client's final sign-off. A project never proceeds to print without the client sign-off, and it is the client who has the final responsibility for work at this stage of the process.

In the case of print collateral, Voice supplies the finished art to the printer and takes responsibility for receiving and checking printer's proofs for every job before printing proceeds. Clients also have the option to sign off on printer's proofs. The final stage of the process is the press check, which Voice undertakes to ensure quality control of the print. The print quality in terms of colors, paper stock, and registration is monitored and the printed sheets are checked to ensure that they are free from imperfections.

Case Study in Organizing and Persuading:

Voice / Adelaide, Australia

Longview Vineyard

Longview is a stunning, family-owned vineyard located just outside the historic township of Macclesfield in the Adelaide Hills. Set on undulating slopes reminiscent of classic Old World estates, it has quickly established itself as one of the most awarded vineyards in the region since its first vintage in 2001. In 2008, Voice was commissioned to relabel some of Longview's premium wines.

BELOW
"The clients, brothers Peter and Mark Saturno, had never worked with a designer before, so we had to work extremely hard to get them to have confidence in Voice, the design process, and fee structure," says Carslake. "Once they were committed, we went about the process a little differently: After numerous field trips to the vineyard, wine tastings, open discussions, and so on, we presented three concepts for the labels:

- The first one took exactly what they wanted according to their brief.
- The second one took their brief a little further.
- The third one represented what we thought was best and where we wanted to take them.

When we presented our third concept, they couldn't go back to what they thought they wanted in the brief. In this way, we gained their confidence by doing what they asked, and then by taking them to a place they couldn't imagine. The approach worked brilliantly for this client and illustrated the value of working with designers. Longview has come a long way, and they now have very high expectations of Voice and the concepts we develop. It is a great relationship, as we are always being challenged and looking forward to the next project."

Back Label

In Australia, cleanskin is a term for bottled wine that doesn't carry a label or any other identifying marks. Cleanskin wines are sold in sealed cartons of six or twelve bottles, and the carton must display a label that meets the minimum legal requirements as defined by Australian law. "Cleanskin wines have been sold in Australia since at least the early 1960s, but they are generally popular only during periods of imbalance in the Australian domestic wine market," says De Leo.

"Wineries will sell cleanskins to dump excess or unwanted wine stocks and do so to avoid the negative consequences of discounting their existing brands." This form of dumping often has very little to do with the quality of the wine. In 2009, Back Label commissioned Voice to design a label for its cleanskin.

"The perception and value of the design industry changes when clients realize they need design expertise and they actually experience the design process with a designer."
—Anthony De Leo, codirector, Voice

LEFT
Cleanskin wines are characterized by their very low price, a simple paper label, and the fact that they can be purchased as individual bottles. "Typically, there is no budget," explains Carslake. "Labels are generally printed on an in-house laser printer at each winery, labeled, packed, and sent to retail stores. With Back Label, the client wanted to see what we could do for a minimal fee, but they were not expecting anything of real value." The resultant graphics are visually arresting and took the idea of a cleanskin label to a new place.

Case Study in Organizing and Persuading:

Voice / Adelaide, Australia

Type It Write

Now in its second edition, Voice's own product, called *Type It Write*, is an indispensable reference guide to punctuation geared toward designers. To foster clearer and more effective communication, this book addresses the usage of the most common forms of punctuation, including apostrophes, commas, quotation marks, and semicolons, and provides valuable guidance about matters such as emphasis, placing punctuation with quotation marks, and preparing lists.

"All graphic design studios are presented with copy from clients to be typeset," notes Carslake. "How well this copy is prepared varies, and so does the expectation on the graphic designer to double as an editor. We started to notice that with every job we

produced, we were cleaning up punctuation mistakes and inconsistencies in supplied copy. We became frustrated with the repetitive process of proofing and editing supplied copy, not least because as designers, editing was not our primary skill, but also because it became obvious that copy prepared correctly in the first place would save us and our clients a lot of time." Out of this need, Voice produced a guide to punctuation that could be supplied to clients as a reference tool when writing copy to be typeset.

The second edition of *Type It Write* introduces additional topics, such as the use of acronyms and italics, and places more emphasis on usage examples. The book is more exciting visually and even easier to use than the first edition.

BELOW AND OPPOSITE
After years of being continually asked if there were any spare copies floating around the studio, Voice knew it was time to edit and print a second edition. "Over time, *Type It Write* has attracted the interest of people from various industries; we regularly receive emails about the book and get specific feedback on some of the finer details of punctuation and grammar," says Carslake. Voice will also create customized editions of the publication that are branded and follow specific corporate style standards for companies with more than 250 staff members. More details are available at www.typeitwrite.com.au.

Apostrophes

Apostrophes are used for the following reasons:

· to show possession

One boy's dream.
The Jones' house.

Tip: the apostrophe is placed after the name of the owner or possessor.
Who owns the dream? The boy does.
Who owns the house? The Jones family.

· to indicate time

It was a hard day's work.

How long did the work go for? A day.

· to indicate the omission of figures in dates

I was born in September '76.

· to show the plural of single letters

Dot the i's and cross the t's.

· to indicate the omission of letters.

It's = It is

Who's = Who is
They're = They are

Common errors

✗ The dog pulled at it's collar.
✔ The dog pulled at its collar.

✗ They're playing at the childrens' playground.
✔ They're playing at the children's playground.

Tip: apostrophes are not used when making plurals.
✗ Come inside for DVD's, CD's and Video's.
✔ Come inside for DVDs, CDs and Videos.

✗ It was successful in/during the 1990's.
✔ It was successful in/during the 1990s.

Tip: make sure you use an apostrophe—not a prime symbol (which looks similar at small sizes, but is used for different units of measurement and other purposes in mathematics).

10

11

Ampersands

An **ampersand** means *and*. They are only used in referencing when citing a list of authors or in organisational names where an ampersand is used officially by the organisation in place of *and*.

The report claims that soccer will become Australia's favourite sport (Heppell, James **&** Dalton 2009).

P**&**O, Mills **&** Boon

Numerals

Common sense prevails when using numerals.

Present dates entirely as numerals or spell out only the month. Make sure you:
· follow the day, month, year sequence
· do not use commas
· write the day as a numeral only without a suffix (i.e. don't use 1st, 2nd, 3rd, etc.).

18/03/09

18 March **2009**

Spell out large numbers, especially in sentences.

One million 1,000,000

Spell out numbers of less than 10. Use numerals for numbers 10 and higher.

It takes **nine** hours, not **12**.

In tables, for a series of numbers or when making comparisons, it is preferable to use numerals, especially when incorporating decimal points.

USD 0.8689
EUR 0.5904
GBP 0.5349
NZD 1.2111

$26,000 in **2008**

$34,000 in **2009**

Tools for Organizing Design

Along with the basic structural blueprints—the creative brief, designer–client agreement, SOW, and process outline—designers can also employ some specific tools to help them organize project work flow. The main objective here is to provide constant communication and oversight of the project. Everyone involved in the design—both the designer's team and the client's—needs to have the project's scope, vision, and goals at hand.

Typically, there are hundreds of details to consider, respond to, incorporate, and handle. Each team member tends to focus only on his or her own piece of the project, so someone has to keep the overall picture in mind. This is the role of the project manager.

Because design firms are often small businesses, it is common to have only one project manager who is responsible for all projects. Therefore, it is not unusual to have a design manager who is sweating the details of specific projects as well as monitoring the firm's overall work flow. Details on top of details present themselves and must be considered and prioritized in a kind of constant triage.

Tracking Documents

To help facilitate the process, project managers should create documentation and tracking tools, including

- A master list of job numbers
- A list of all open jobs with key milestone dates
- Status reports on individual projects
- Detailed schedules on each project
- Team contact information sheets for each project
- Job jackets for each project, both digital and physical
- Gantt charts and calendars plotting all open job deadlines
- Billing status reports on all projects
- Time sheets for all team members
- Progress reports that chart hours worked by team members
- Purchase orders to track project-related expenses
- Expense reports for out-of-pocket costs
- Income projections

The objective is to create useful information that helps manage the process. There are myriad ways to accomplish this; choose the one that provides the most useful information, and that is easy to implement and update. Project managers can add layers of complexity to the information recorded, thereby making tons of work for themselves. For some firms, this might be necessary; for others, it's not. Use trial and error and do what works best for your firm. The only certainty is that having no documentation is a recipe for disaster. Something somewhere will inevitably be forgotten or missed.

Forecasting the Work

To better manage the work in a design firm you need to keep two lists:

1. Open Jobs

This is a list of all projects you have committed to. These jobs have signed designer–client agreements and are in some stage of progress. If the list includes your fees for the projects, the document becomes an accounts receivable list. If you specify the month you expect to receive payments, you have an income projection document. When the projects on the list include a note regarding what stage the work is in, the list becomes a status report. Make sure to open a unique job number for each project, even for house jobs. Update the open jobs list frequently.

2. Potential Work

This is a list of possible jobs. List projects that clients have talked about but haven't requested an estimate for. Also list all proposals that are pending client approval. Here again, adding information such as expected compensation and potential start and completion dates boosts the document's effectiveness as a forecasting tool. Understanding cash flow (the movement of cash in and out of the business), and the need to increase sales and new-business development (because there's no upcoming work) or consider hiring additional staff members (because there's too much work on the horizon), is possible by tracking potential work in an organized way. There is an ebb and flow to all design businesses, but the need for steady income streams is constant. This list allows you to manage that.

DESIGNER AND COMPANY STATUS REPORT
January 2, 2010

CLIENT	JOB #	DESCRIPTION	STATUS
AIGA	AIG357	AIGA Miscellaneous	Ongoing.
BellCorp.	BEL235	Yellow Pages: Phase 1	Need contract and schedule.
	BEL236	Yellow Pages: Phase 2	Proceed upon completion of Phase 1.
	BEL237	Yellow Pages: Phase 3	Proceed upon completion of Phase 2.
	BEL238	Yellow Pages: Phase 4	Proceed upon completion of Phase 3.
Designer & Co.	DCO350	PowerPoint Presentation	Working. Fancy Photographer to shoot interiors.
	DCO351	Newsletter	TLS working. Need layouts 1/15/10.
	DCO352	Proposal Presentation	Need the printed version. Need revised specs.
	DCO353	Misc. Self-promotion	Ongoing.

These charts illustrate three versions of a design firm's status report. The top one is a simple job list with minimal information about the status of work. The bottom right version, which is emailed to the design team, acts as more of a to-do list with more detailed tasks broken down. The bottom left chart is a billing status report in which a project manager provides a bookkeeper with billing information. Any and all of these documents can be used effectively to keep work flowing through a design firm.

DESIGNER AND COMPANY BILLING STATUS REPORT
January 2, 2010

JOB #	CLIENT	STATUS
	AC Architect Partners	
ACA2240	Art College Student Housing Signage	Contract awarded. No work begun. Bill commencement on 1/27/10?
	BellCorp.	
BEL2249	Misc. Production Requests	Bill hourly at end of each month. Last bill: 11/17/09. Next bill: 1/14/10.
BEL2269	Winter Invitations	Work in progress. Billed 50% on 12/24/09. Bill final 3/15/10.
BEL2275	Promo Logo and Guidelines	In progress. Bill phase completions per estimate.
BEL2292	Monthly Guide	In progress. Job will be ongoing. Billed 50% on 12/3/09. Next bill: 1/30/10.
BEL2228	Additional Stationery	Completed. Bill in full: 12/19/09.
BEL2309	PowerPoint Presentation	Completed. Bill in full: 12/19/09.
BEL2314	Collateral Template	Billed remaining expenses 1/8/10.
BEL2348	Fellowship ID	Need estimate.
	Designer & Co.	
DCO439	DCO Time/DCO Admin.	Ongoing. No billing.
DCO9701	Self-Promo	Ongoing. Expect reprint of promo brochure invoice from LithoPrint.
DCO446	Misc. Archiving	Ongoing. Review cost of Cumulus software?
DCO740	General Competition Submissions	Ongoing. Expect entry fees for AIGA 365.
DCO2132	DCO Website	Website at engineer. Expect invoice 2/21/10. Renew hosting contract.
DCO2148	DCO New Business 2010	Proposals out to UCA, LaLa University, Big Deal TV.
DCO2289	TLS trip to Memphis.	Expenses invoiced. Paid?
DCO2301	Blog Updates	Ongoing. No billing.
DCO2325	Felt & Wire DCO Products	Ongoing. Need monthly report.
DCO2320	Purchase Misc. Supplies	Ongoing. Get DJ a DCO credit card per TLS.

PROJECT STATUS 01/01/2010 — INBOX

From:	**Terry Lee Stone**
Subject:	**PROJECT STATUS 01/01/2010**
Date:	**January 2, 2010 4:31:5 7 PM PST**
To:	**Designer Smith, Designer Jones**

PROJECT STATUS 01/01/2010

BellCorp.: BEL2269 Winter Invitations
— February prints done and delivered
— Awaiting text from client on March invites
— Awaiting schedule from client on printing requests

Designer & Co.
Designer & Co. Website: DCO2132
— On hold until Singapore agreement is finalized

Designer & Co. Competition Submission: DCO740
— Need consent from client to show BellCorp. invitations by 1/11
— Need to determine missions for AGA 365 competition
— Richard Smith book submissions due by 1/22

Designer & Co. Archiving/Image Library: DCO446
— DS working on archiving old jobs from 2009
— DW cleaning up image library
— Need to discuss process for organization and searchable database

Designer & Co. Website: DCO270
— DW to schedule George to look at our printer setup
— BellCorp. PowerPoint for TLS: DONE

Job Numbers

There are many ways to number design projects to keep track of them for work flow and billing purposes. Here's a system that works well:

Client Code + Sequential Number

For example:
ABC100 (Job #100 is for ABC Television)
IBM101 (Job #101 is for IBM Corporation)

Identifying jobs this way makes them more memorable than a string of numbers only. It also facilitates filing physical job jackets and paperwork by client. It is important to open or create job numbers for each and every job in house, even the firm's self-initiated projects.

The Advantages of Time Sheets

Another essential tool that well-run design firms use is the time sheet, which records how designers spend their workday. By breaking the workday into fifteen-minute increments, recording the tasks done, and assigning this time to an open job number, designers provide managers with important information that affects the project, and the firm's overall health and wealth.

Time sheets
- Tell designers how they spent their time
- Record actual work on jobs
- Help determine profitability
- Assist in accurate billing
- Give employers an understanding of the staff's efficiency
- Allow employees to justify their salaries
- Alert project managers to time/budget issues on jobs
- Inform hiring decisions and capacity planning
- Provide a means of more accurate scoping and pricing on future projects

Project management software requires diligent updates by the project manager and consistent data input by the design team to keep the information accurate and up to date. As with everything, there are pros and cons to using a software solution.

Some of the pros of design project management software:
- It affords good information sharing among multiple team members, particularly virtual teams.
- It provides a central hub for all information and records.
- Dynamic changes to the information are possible and easy.
- Web-based solutions allow access to the information wherever and whenever the team needs it.
- It provides a perception of order and thorough management, which can be impressive to executives in a design firm, and to clients if they have access.
- It assists in workforce management, creating records for costs, paid and unpaid time off, vacations, attendance, and skills assessment.

Some of the cons of design project management software:
- The information may be inaccurate if it is not constantly updated.
- Some programs put too much emphasis on tasks and milestones, and not enough on overall project goals and parameters.
- Many "all-in-one" solutions don't allow for a look at estimated versus actual time on a project.
- Few, if any, solutions have good invoicing and accounting capabilities.

When selecting design project management software, look for programs that
- Are Web-based
- Are easy to learn and use
- Allow for collaboration
- Have features you will actually use

Case Study in Project Setup:

AtelierWorks / London, UK

Headed by designers Ian Chilvers, John Powner, and Quentin Newark, AtelierWorks is a graphic design studio specializing in branding. "AtelierWorks is a name that expresses our firm," says Chilvers. "An 'atelier' is a place where artists work, a place of imagination. A 'works' houses efficient modern industry. We combine imagination and effectiveness in our practice." The studio produces a range of branded materials for a variety of clients. Its process, however, remains the same: research, conceive, develop, execute, and appraise. It is a systematic approach that serves AtelierWorks well.

Volkswagen

Both Volkswagen (VW) and Audi cars had been sold in the same showrooms for years. However, as the market expanded it became necessary to separate the brands and redesign the showroom and collateral materials. The Volkswagen Retail Concept (VRC) was created in Germany. VRC laid down the basic principles for a new showroom environment and the United Kingdom was to lead the way in implementing the strategy. It was also seen as an opportunity to change the way dealers worked. Dealers were to become retailers, putting customers' interests first. Over five years, AtelierWorks worked closely with a small but important set of VW marketing staff members, external design managers, suppliers, and architects. The goal was to unify all the VW activities and materials so that every new marketing initiative built on the success of the previous one.

"The dilemma faced when developing any corporate merchandise range is the task of producing something a customer would actually want," says Chilvers. "Inspiration was drawn directly from high street fashion labels. It seems obvious now, but this had never really been done before." Previous branded merchandise was more about promoting a VW logo than generating an understated "must have" product. AtelierWorks made the VW branding elements much more discreet. Like the corporate merchandise, the accessory packaging had also ignored the high street. Some items were supplied from the factory in Germany, but much of it came from other outside sources. The result was an uncoordinated display in the new showroom.

What sort of showroom suits a Volkswagen car

is it:

a) the best bunting money can buy

or

b) thoughtful design with no gimmicks?

The strength of VRC is its clarity and simplicity. It creates a place for everything, so everything can be in its place. The colonnade provides a series of 'slots', which can take both graphic panels and other units.

Everything is very much on show. Customers can find what they're looking for without needing to go up to a counter and ask. The design works for them because the layout is so clear. The design works for the retailer because it puts no barriers between customers and their decision to buy a car.

This no-fuss arrangement mirrors the honest design of Volkswagen cars. There are no visual distractions which lessen the impact of the cars. Everything customers see in the showroom increases their sense of Volkswagen quality, the feeling that brought them through the door in the first place.

Wheels

Vantage

More Volkswagen for your money

2001 model year

Prices effective from 01.07.00 to 30.09.00

Volkswagen Solutions

You can depend on it

$$X = \int_{\frac{\pi}{2}}^{\cos x} \left\{ \frac{1}{x} e^{\sin x} y \right\}_0^1$$

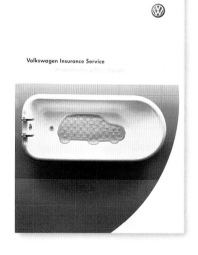

Volkswagen Insurance Service

ABOVE AND OPPOSITE
Elements such as signs, point-of-sale pieces, vehicle presentations, paperwork, merchandise, and packaging were areas of the business that (at the time) were approached differently in every country because they were subject to regional legislation and cultural attitudes.

AtelierWorks was tasked with making the VW brand connect with the UK consumer. These initial package designs, below, were developed to be applied to both factory and outside supplier products. They feature clear labeling, color-coded ranges, and humorous imagery.

Case Study in Project Setup:

AtelierWorks / London, UK

King's College London

King's College London is one of the oldest and largest colleges of the University of London. The school is one of the top academic institutions of its kind in Europe, yet it had an identity issue that AtelierWorks helped to solve. "They own much of the south façade of The Strand [a historical street in Central London], and yet no one knew it," says Chilvers. "We proposed a timeline that plots every year since King's founding in 1829." Each year presents significant alumni—from the Duke of Wellington to the Reverend Desmond Tutu, and right up to the present day (a language student named Magdelena Jackiewicz).

BELOW
The design incorporates large portraits of key figures in the history of King's College. "The timeline unifies the various architectural styles and treatments of the façade and gives several messages about King's: We own all this; we provoke thought; we have produced significant world-changing students; we still do, and hope to continue this in the future," explains Chilvers.

The 623 foot (190 m) frontage along the River Thames defines the territory of King's College. It is outward-facing and addresses a wider public than the client imagined possible when they first asked AtelierWorks to look at signing their buildings. The effect is an enormous branding experience that is also a history lesson for passersby. "This is sign work as branding. This is branding reaching out to the public," says Chilvers.

Royal Geographic Society

The Royal Geographical Society (RGS) was founded in 1830 for the advancement of geographical sciences. The society has an eminent history—with explorers such as David Livingstone, Ernest Shackleton, and Sir Edmund Hillary, all having researched and lectured on their travels to the society's fellows in the wood-paneled lecture hall. This previously dusty and remote body was in need of modernization. Beginning with a full brand audit and culminating in a set of guidelines, the RGS then decided to retain AtelierWorks' services. Over a five-year period, AtelierWorks redesigned all of the RGS communications and continues to do so. This ongoing relationship has brought continuity to the brand.

BELOW LEFT AND CENTER
The challenge for AtelierWorks was to design materials that appeal to the widest possible audience range, making the important subject of geography relevant to young and old alike. Colorful graphics and provocative imagery pull the viewer into this fascinating area of study. The RGS logo is based on map typography. "We have used a globelike disc as the focus for all imagery," notes Chilvers. "The disc is also an identifier and an element that works in 3-D for things like signs, and in the digital world for websites."

BELOW
The website appeals to both new audiences and those familiar with RGS. With more than 15,000 members, the society is the largest and most active of the world's scholarly geographical societies. It is a leading world center for geographic learning—supporting education, teaching, research, and scientific expeditions, as well as promoting public understanding and enjoyment of geography.

Leaving a lasting legacy
Shape our future world

Royal Geographical Society
with IBG

Advancing geography and geographical learning

● Help us reach our target of a £10 million endowment to fund education, expeditions, research and the public engagement with geography

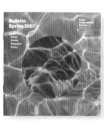
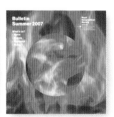

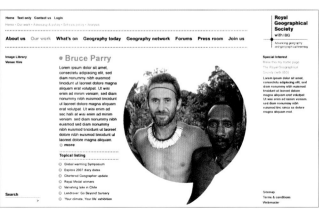

Persuasion and Project Management

Every design project requires a guide who will be responsible for making sure the design team delivers on the client's expectations. This role passes through several phases, and requires different skills depending on the project's status:

- Leader: commanding the respect of the client and design team
- Manager: actively participating in and guiding the process
- Monitor: overseeing and being accountable for the project's status
- Mentor: advising, counseling, and maybe even training team members
- Enforcer: compelling compliance and ensuring that things happen as required

Another important aspect of setting up a design project is empowering the person acting as project manager. Typically, a project manager is not the team members' actual "boss." Even if the entire team agrees in theory, in practice, they aren't always easy to manage. Powerful persuasion skills used right from the start, and then applied throughout the project lifecycle, is critically important for any project manager.

Because the project manager is a functional lead in terms of getting the work done, and is often speaking to the various stakeholders, including the client, on a near-daily basis, the project manager needs to persuade people to trust him or her.

METHODS OF PERSUASION
This chart provides six methods of persuading people. You can use these concepts on your design team to manage projects, or with clients to manage the working relationship, particularly for getting approval on design solutions.

Reason

Persuasion can be achieved using
- Previous agreement
- Logical argument
- Valid premise
- Critical arrangements
- Truth statements

Rhetoric

Persuasion can be achieved using
- Compelling language
- Intriguing discourse
- Authoritative style
- Lively conversation
- Shared interpretations

Science

Persuasion can be achieved using
- Undisputed facts
- Empirical evidence
- Quantifiable results
- Measurable data
- Repeatable steps

Emotion

Persuasion can be achieved by
- Instilling confidence
- Leveraging fear
- Inducing happiness
- Eliciting trust
- Generating feelings

Imagination

Persuasion can be achieved by
- Leveraging belief
- Invoking faith
- Perceiving value
- Forming sensations
- Envisioning potential

Affinity

Persuasion can be achieved by
- Befriending personally
- Inducing camaraderie
- Invoking community
- Enticing
- Boosting team spirit

Managing by Persuasion

Human nature being what it is, many well-intentioned designers go off track or procrastinate when a job becomes difficult. Poor planning and bad organization can lead to all kinds of things that derail a project. The goal here is to keep things progressing toward the client's objectives. This is where the fine art of persuasion can be leveraged to great effect.

In this context, persuasion means influencing, guiding, and inducing someone to do or believe in something. However, creativity is elusive. Sometimes creativity is hard work, and even a well-intentioned, experienced designer can get bogged down. A project manager needs to help get designers back to the task. Being demanding or threatening rarely, if ever, works, so persuasion and even salesmanship need to be employed.

Motivating the Team

Design project managers bounce between being a designer's best friend and his or her worst nightmare. As long as things keep flowing and the work is getting done, everything is all sunshine and roses. But when things become confused or are done incorrectly, or when deadlines are missed, project managers must lay down the law and get things right again.

Project managers must be able to motivate, inform, encourage, and enable the design team. Some designers work for the pure love of design. Some work for fame and glory. Still others are in it for the money. Therefore, the tactics to use when persuading members of a design team to meet their responsibilities and make great work will vary among teams. What will remain constant, however, is the fact that whoever is managing the design team and/or the client needs to be credible from day one. His or her authority, expertise, and functional proficiency need to be unquestioned to garner respect, trust, and empowerment.

The following ideas can be put into action to boost credibility:

- **Exhibit competence:**
  Be prepared for meetings, calls, questions, and problems.

- **Be confident:**
  Speak clearly and trust yourself, your team, and your process.

- **Showcase your track record:**
  Cite examples, talk about case studies, and prove that you have relevant experience.

- **Keep emotions in check:**
  Remain calm, and keep a clear head and an even hand.

- **Don't lie:**
  Even small inauthenticities can spoil your reputation.

- **Deliver on time and on budget:**
  Managers aren't typically responsible for the quality of the design; that is the domain of the creative director. But they are in charge of schedule and cost containment.

Meet these commitments and you will win lasting credibility.
By the way, these things apply to boosting credibility with your clients as well.

25 Tips for Design Project Managers

1. Know and understand the project's goals.
2. Have clear roles and responsibilities.
3. Define success criteria.
4. Get process methodology approved upfront.
5. Build in time for quality control.
6. Negotiate achievable commitments.
7. Keep communication open and up to date.
8. Maintain the schedule, or notify everyone of changes in the timeline.
9. Readjust the process/plan based on progress.
10. Maintain a clear grasp on reality.

13. Course-correct before problems escalate.

14. Separate the people from the problem.

15. Invent options for mutual satisfaction and gain.

16. Be honest and respectful.

17. Keep it moving, take action, and don't delay.

18. Delegate, delegate, delegate.

19. Respect the team's learning curve.

20. Stay flexible.

21. Have a contingency plan.

22. Do the best you can with what you've got.

23. Learn from your mistakes.

24. Say you are sorry and mean it.

25. Learn from your mistakes: do a postproject evaluation.

Project Profile in Project Setup:

House Styling magazine designed by Good Design Company / Tokyo, Japan

House Styling Magazine

Founded in 1999 by art director/president Manabu Mizuno, Good Design Company is a multidisciplined design firm based in Ebisu, the design hub of Tokyo. It creates advertising, product planning tools, print projects, books, identity packages, package design, and interior design for a variety of Japanese and international brands. The firm also does retail and furniture design. Good Design Company worked with *House Styling* magazine for several years developing cover graphics and furniture products.

BELOW
Covers for 2004, 2005, and 2006 issues of *House Styling* feature images of young people in sleek, modern environments. The magazine paired lush photos of rooms with a catalog-like selection of individual home décor pieces, from furniture to lighting to linens. This type of publication is sometimes referred to as a magalog.

BELOW, TOP
Good Design Company's furniture designs were sold through *House Styling*. Its work captures a contemporary yet classic elegance that is at once international and uniquely Japanese.

BELOW, BOTTOM
House Styling offered readers editorial content mixed with glimpses of the environments favored by Japanese tastemakers and celebrities. The graphics support the idea that this magazine assists readers in understanding how to put together and accessorize their homes.

Salesmanship

One important aspect of persuasion in design is sales. Whether it's receiving approval on a design solution or securing a deadline extension, getting your way may take a bit of selling. Of course, one element of salesmanship is all about showmanship: a dazzling and compelling performance. However, the best salesmanship in design occurs in the form of quiet persuasion, when the client doesn't feel you are selling them something. Rather, your suggestions seem to be a logical, inevitable, and desirable outcome.

Any designer can learn from a great salesperson. Here are some things that effective salespeople do that might help a design manager:

- Have a clear objective.
- Do their homework.
- Have good timing.
- Stay in the moment.
- Use relevant triggers.
- Present persuasively.
- Listen and respond.
- Enjoy negotiating.
- Connect with others.
- Use visual aids.
- Aren't afraid to use charm.
- Keep their eyes on the prize (the clear objective).
- Don't take things personally.
- Know when to call it quits.
- Rise up and do it all over again.

Chapter 3
Planning

Design Planning 101

Planning is the intellectual, psychological, and tactical process of thinking about each task that needs to be accomplished to meet a goal. For most designers, broadly speaking, the goal or plan is completion of a great design on time and on budget that meets or exceeds the client's expectations.

The creative brief and the designer–client agreement are useful and practical planning frameworks for design. Both include an initial look at the scope of work (SOW) and examine work process methodology. Both could suffice as planning for most designers.

This chapter will discuss design planning in more detail. We'll see how a designer executes on the creative brief and meets the obligations outlined in the designer–client agreement. We'll also discuss how to look ahead to the planning horizon and how, with practice and dedication, a design manager can forecast and plan fairly accurately.

Work Breakdown Structures

Okay, you've won the client's business, been awarded a project, and completed some basic documentation. Now it's time to break down all aspects of the work required and put them into a work breakdown structure (WBS).

A WBS is a dynamic tool used to describe and define a group's work elements or tasks on a project. The U.S. Department of Defense developed the concept in the 1950s, along with the Program Evaluation and Review Technique (PERT), to create military weaponry, and it has greatly influenced all business and project management theory. The WBS is typically visualized as a branching or tree root diagram that shows a structure's hierarchy—with a top item that branches down into subitems, and into further detailed sub-subitems below it. The diagram shows how things are connected to each other.

Level 1	Level 2	Level 3
Project Name		
	Task or Component 1	
		Subtask or Subcomponent 1 Work Package 1.1
		Subtask or Subcomponent 2 Work Package 1.2
		Subtask or Subcomponent 3 Work Package 1.3
	Task or Component 2	
		Subtask or Subcomponent 1 Work Package 2.1
		Subtask or Subcomponent 2 Work Package 2.2
		Subtask or Subcomponent 3 Work Package 2.3

Here's how to plan a WBS for a design project:
Level 1: State the end goal (typically the project name).
Level 2: List the project's manageable components or tasks. Further identify the subcomponents or tasks (called a work package by professional project managers) that fall under each level 2 item.
Level 3: Show the detailed steps by which each component or task will be created or achieved.

In the WBS list, add only the things that are in the SOW contracted by the client. This is sometimes referred to as the 100% rule: The WBS includes 100 percent of the work defined by the project scope.

WBS: List
In list form, work could look like this. If lists suffice for the team, stop there. You have a useful tool that fully describes the work to be done. However, designers are visual people, and perhaps it makes sense to create a traditional WBS diagram.

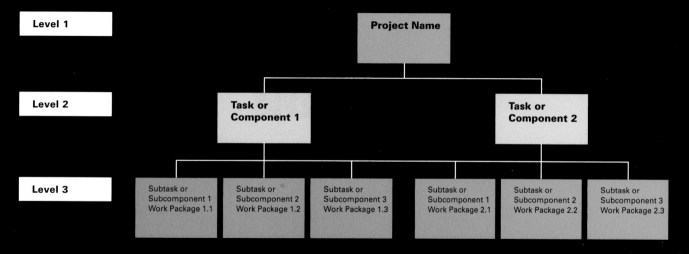

WBS: Diagram

Design project managers can keep amending the diagram, deleting and adding components or tasks as the project progresses. These diagrams can be created with charting or project management software easily. Alternatively, designers can custom-make a WBS diagram for the design team. If a diagram such as this helps to smooth the work flow, make one.

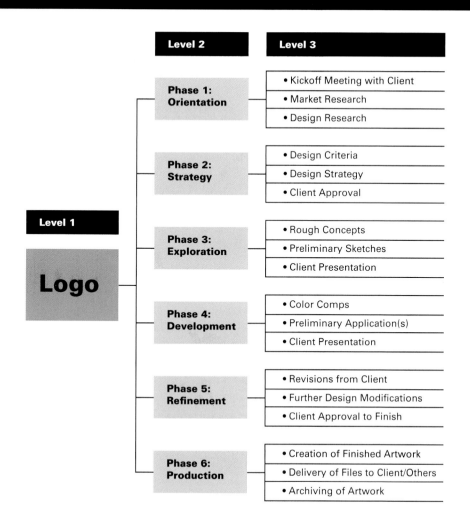

Level 2	Level 3
Phase 1: Orientation	• Kickoff Meeting with Client • Market Research • Design Research
Phase 2: Strategy	• Design Criteria • Design Strategy • Client Approval
Phase 3: Exploration	• Rough Concepts • Preliminary Sketches • Client Presentation
Phase 4: Development	• Color Comps • Preliminary Application(s) • Client Presentation
Phase 5: Refinement	• Revisions from Client • Further Design Modifications • Client Approval to Finish
Phase 6: Production	• Creation of Finished Artwork • Delivery of Files to Client/Others • Archiving of Artwork

Level 1

Logo

WBS for a Logo Design

This is a WBS diagram for a simple logo project. The WBS could also contain a level 4 that identifies the tasks required to accomplish the major milestones listed in level 3. A WBS can break down the work to the finest detail, or it can provide more of an overview as this chart does. A further refinement would be to add due dates and even assign a person responsible for doing the work. Each person on the project may then wish to create his or her own work breakdown either as a diagram or as a simple to-do list.

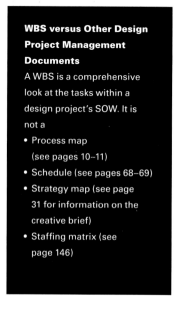

WBS versus Other Design Project Management Documents

A WBS is a comprehensive look at the tasks within a design project's SOW. It is not a

• Process map
  (see pages 10–11)
• Schedule (see pages 68–69)
• Strategy map (see page 31 for information on the creative brief)
• Staffing matrix (see page 146)

Scheduling Design

After everyone understands the work to be done, the next aspect of planning to address is scheduling. Sometimes in design, the only two clear dates are the day the client gives approval to start the job and the day they want the work delivered. Some clients might also specify a few key dates in between, but typically the onus is on the designer to develop due dates and milestones for each phase of the project.

Creating a Flexible Framework

Design project managers must understand that scheduling is an ongoing, dynamic activity. It is rare for a design project to follow the initial schedule exactly. Dates slip and slide for several reasons, mostly related to the client (e.g., the client doesn't provide a vital piece of information required to proceed, fails to sign off on some work, or

makes additional changes). If a manager thinks of scheduling as a flexible framework, but is very clear on which deadlines must not be missed, he or she will run a saner project.

To facilitate scheduling, communication between the design team and the client must clearly spell out responsibilities and critical requirements. The client also must understand that any missed deadlines on their part will affect all subsequent due dates and deadlines. It's pretty much a cardinal rule for a graphic design firm not to miss any deadlines; clients can miss deadlines, but designers cannot. If a deadline issue arises, it is best to alert the client as early as possible that there is a problem and the work will be late. It's all about managing client expectations and satisfaction.

The diagram below provides an overview of the design scheduling process. It is helpful for a project manager to clearly understand what is required for each phase of work. A big mistake is to tell the design team to begin work without all the elements they need to do the work. This problem is compounded when promises to the client are made regarding due dates, based on that misinformation. A formal scheduling and planning process improves logistics, avoids wasted time, and helps the team stay on track.

Design Project Scheduling Process

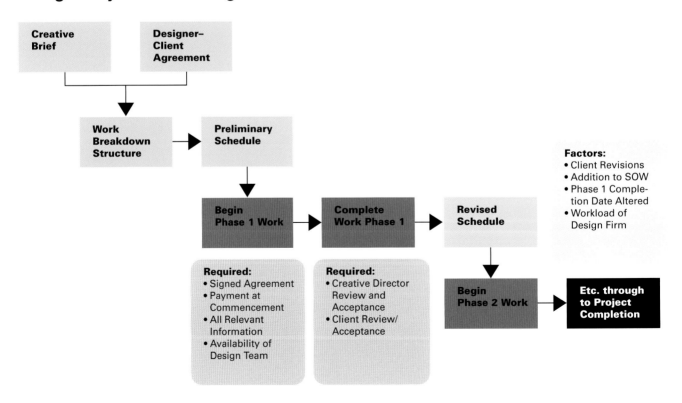

Creating Gantt Charts for Design Projects

Scheduling is challenging due to the ever-changing nature of design. In scheduling projects, consider which tasks and activities must be performed sequentially and which are discrete activities, meaning they do not depend on prior tasks being completed. To help visualize the interdependencies of all the components and tasks in a design project, as well as to map them to a time schedule, designers can create a Gantt chart.

A Gantt chart (see diagram below) is a classic project management tool that shows multiple tasks and timelines in a single document. Typically, time is noted in weeks or days and is placed on the horizontal axis. A list of tasks is placed as the vertical axis. Solid bars indicate where each task falls in the timeline, and its duration.

It is not essential to create a Gantt chart for every design project; a simple list of due dates, followed by an email reminder, may work perfectly for some teams. For others, especially if they are using project management or spreadsheet software, diagrams are easy to make and very useful because they are clear, visual, and efficient.

Reasons for Noncompliance

H. Glen Ballard, Ph.D., cofounder of the Lean Construction Institute, an organization dedicated to project management, and professor at the University of California/Berkeley and Stanford University, notes ten reasons scheduled activities don't occur as planned.

1. Lack of decision
2. Lack of prerequisites
3. Lack of resources
4. Priority change(s)
5. Insufficient time
6. Late start
7. Conflicting demands
8. Acts of God
9. Project changes
10. Other

Ballard recommends noting the reasons for noncompliance by number in communication documents with clients.

Gantt Chart for Phase 1 of a Logo Design

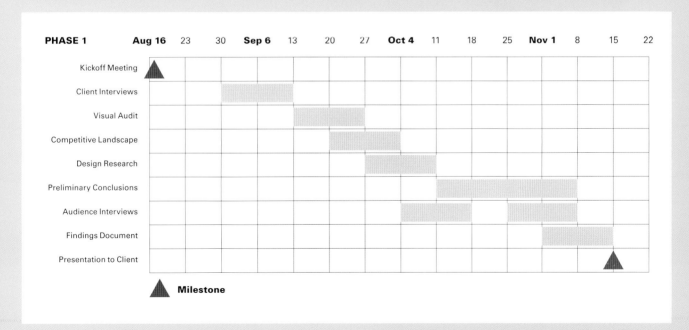

Milestone

This Gantt chart maps out phase 1 of a logo design project. It is an at-a-glance look at the schedule for the major work activities which must be performed in the initial stages of this project. For a look at the WBS diagram for this type of project, turn to page 66.

Case Study in Planning:

Haus Design Communications / Los Angeles, California USA

Haus Design Communications serves the network society by creating exciting branding for the Internet, mobile phones, social media, and print and broadcast media. "We walk the interconnected paths of this new world," says creative director Rasmus Blaesbjerg. "We can't help it; it's something we were born into." Blaesbjerg, together with partners Jared Plummer and Morten Bay, are interested in producing work that is authentic, multicultural, and emotional. They provide brand strategy and stewardship, media consultation, animation, publishing concepts, design, live action and motion graphics, and business development for a variety of client categories. All of their work requires meticulous planning and attention to detail due to the complex nature of their projects.

LA Magazine Circle

Los Angeles, an affluent-lifestyle magazine, wanted to represent the same concept in the online world. Its readers, especially the younger ones, were migrating to online content, and the magazine's goal was to extend its reach and connect with readers there as well. Haus redesigned lamag.com, capturing the sensibility of the print version of the publication but strategically optimizing the website in ways that would also make money—from placing nonintrusive sponsored ad space to creating the Circles club concept.

ABOVE

Los Angeles Circles is a social club that offers members discounts on great experiences, and unique deals for free. Having one of the most affluent and attractive readerships in the United States allows the magazine to give Circles members access to restaurants, businesses, movie theaters, spas, museums, and resorts.

ABOVE

It's no small task to design websites to accommodate information-heavy content, but Haus created an inviting and highly visual design for *Los Angeles* magazine's Circles club. On this project, the designers were business consultants as well as designers. In fact, it was Haus who recommended development of the Circles concept.

Paige Black Label

Paige Black Label is a division of Paige Premium Denim LLC, a clothing company founded in 2004 by fit model Paige Adams-Geller on the principle that women don't have to be a tiny size to look and feel great in clothes. Haus worked with Geller to create a distinctive presence for this sophisticated line of women's pants, tops, dresses, skirts, and outerwear.

BELOW
Dominated by black, the Paige Black Label website's home page features a dreamy animation. A beautiful shell opens, exploding into fragments of subtle color and texture that seem to float like a dream across the screen, resolving into a catalog navigation strip at the bottom. From there, Haus's design directs viewers to simple, elegant product pages.

"We'll admit it: We're geeks. Rather than being smart ad men in dark designer suits, we are nerds who have found a way to use our love of gadgets, computers, and the online world to help others obtain commercial success. Basically, we just love to play around anything that has a screen and is connected."
—Rasmus Blaesbjerg, creative director, Haus

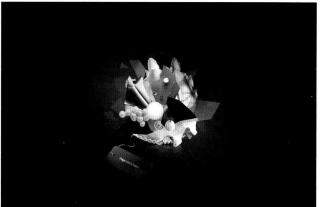

Case Study in Planning:

Haus Design Communications / Los Angeles, California USA

Isaora

Isaora is a line of snowboard-inspired advanced sportswear that proves that technical performance and progressive style are not mutually exclusive. Haus worked with Isaora to develop its branding, website, and *Look Book*, which previews the products to the press and to retailers. Both Isaora and Haus are obsessed by design, and carefully crafted a variety of materials and images to attract adventure seekers who also happen to be fashionistas.

BELOW

Isaora products provide real style, performance, and protection for the people who wear them, and Haus's graphics convey these truths. "In this densely connected media world, and on the globalized infinite store shelf of the Web, there is always something more believable within reach," notes Haus executive producer Jared Plummer. "That's why, at Haus, we focus on distilling the essence of a product or brand so that the authenticity stands out. Impenetrable. Anytime, anywhere."

PBS / *Behind Closed Doors: Stalin, the Nazis, and the West*

Los Angeles PBS television affiliate KCET engaged Haus to create a Web presence for its PBS documentary miniseries *Behind Closed Doors: Stalin, the Nazis, and the West*. The website presents never-before-seen facts and material, which had been under lock and key in Russian archives since World War II. Haus incorporated a plethora of images and text in an educational, appealing, and entertaining manner.

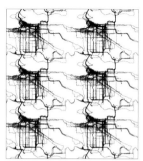
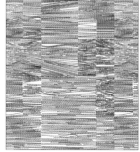

ABOVE AND OPPOSITE

"The big challenge here was creating an architecture that would make it easy to understand and navigate an information-heavy website," explains Blaesbjerg. "Our solution was to focus on the three leaders in question: Stalin, Churchill, and Roosevelt." Maps, coupled with videos and witness stories throughout the site, create a lively presentation. "Our design lets the rich imagery speak for itself," Blaesbjerg says. "The whole site looks transported from another time."

Case Study in Planning:

Haus Design Communications / Los Angeles, California USA

Chad Allen Magic

Working with magician Chad Allen was Haus's first personality branding assignment. "Allen is a blind magician, which in itself sounds like something out of a freak show," explains Blaesbjerg. "When you meet the man, feel his charisma, and enjoy the incredible magic he performs, you realize how he embodies perseverance and will power that is quite inspiring." The branding and website Haus created for Allen immediately give viewers a strong sense of who this magician really is.

"We took magic's classic symbols—the club, the rabbit, the hat, the playing card—and placed them in a different environment: nature," explains Blaesbjerg. "By connecting the emotions of nature's wonders to the wonders of magic, we created the notion that real magic is not what happens on stage but within us."

"Haus focuses on creating emotional experiences in communication. With our human branding efforts, we're working to revolutionize how truly charismatic people can connect emotionally with consumers."
—Jared Plummer,
    executive producer, Haus

OPPOSITE

The website works to embody the concept of inspiration and charisma which Chad Allen possesses. Haus's branding for the magician has worked wonders for his career. It has also helped make him an influential spokesperson for disabled people on Capitol Hill and in the White House—powerful U.S. government entities. In addition, it has supported Allen in his work as an inspirational speaker and performer.

BELOW

Allen's website emphasizes fun and an educational twist on magic. He's an expert performer in magic and illusion, even though he is blind. The site graphics are mysterious and intriguing, pulling the viewer into Allen's unique world. His completely different take on classic magician repertoires is conveyed through imagery that is slightly askew.

Scheduling Simple versus Complex Projects

Simple projects, such as creating a promotional flyer for a retail store, tend to happen quickly, have few components, have fewer people involved, and likely have lower stakes. Complex projects, such as creating a website for that same retail store, mean scheduling multiple tasks that are likely done by multiple team members (e.g., the person writing the copy is rarely programming the site) and are vitally important to the basic commercial aspects of the store, so the stakes are high.

Since work on complex projects requires coordination and completion of certain activities before others can begin, it's a good idea to develop a fine-tuned schedule in which each task, activity, and corresponding deadline is assigned to a specific team member to ensure that the work gets done.

The following are critical components when scheduling large projects:

- ▶ Clear tasks and deadlines
- ▶ Assignment of responsibility
- ▶ Procedures for dealing with changes
- ▶ Tracking and reporting process
- ▶ Oversight management
- ▶ Central Web-based calendar
- ▶ Frequent schedule updates

Project Profile in Planning:
FreedomWig 2 designed by Martha Rich

FreedomWig 2

Illustrator Martha Rich decided to create a regularly scheduled self-promotional website called FreedomWig. The site presents one painting per day, which can be purchased directly from the website. "I needed something to keep me busy during down times," explains Rich. "I tend to be lazy and do better when I have to be accountable to something. Originally, I made a pact with myself to post one painting a day for a year, and then I kept going." Her paintings feature her own wacky vocabulary of images inspired by everything from vintage women's magazines to restaurant menus.

FreedomWig has a simple interface that allows viewers to see and enjoy Rich's paintings. Her work exhibits a kind of charming naiveté coupled with sassy social commentary on the lives of women in general, and Rich's own personal experience. Her work has appeared in numerous magazines, including *McSweeney's* and *Nylon*, as well as in gallery shows and exhibitions.

Rich came to illustration after holding various jobs, including fast-food worker and corporate cubicle slave. She took night classes, eventually enrolling in art school, and most recently pursuing her master's degree in grad school. Her distinctive voice, with its well-earned raw edges, stands out in a world dominated by pleasantly suitable illustration styles.

"The strength of Rich's visual language results in raw, edgy, and sometimes disturbing images," says design journalist Matthew Porter. "She communicates a heightened sense of irony, a byproduct of her amusement with life, for better or for worse. In short, Rich's work is informed by her experiences, but unlike some, she never really imagined her story would inform any art, much less her own."

Time Management

Strictly speaking, time management is an ongoing activity that all team members must engage in throughout a design project. However, it is an issue to address upfront in the planning of a design project as well. When scoping the work (see page 40) and then creating a thorough WBS (page 66), the project manager knows exactly what will be done and the hierarchical nature of the tasks (if relevant). He or she has also determined approximately how much time it will take to complete the tasks and has committed all of this information into a schedule. This is great in theory, but will it work in reality? This is where time management checks and balances are helpful in staging a job and staying on track with the projected work flow.

Designers Need Time Sheets

The best tool to aid in time management is time sheets, which record in fifteen-minute intervals what a designer is doing during his or her workday. Many designers resist this practice—mostly because it is tedious. Some also believe time sheets are irrelevant if a project has a fixed fee, instead of being billed hourly. That is a short-sighted notion. Time sheets are extremely valuable because they are an essential tool for ensuring profitability and estimating future work.

Time sheets allow design managers to track the team's progress. By reviewing time sheets on an ongoing basis (daily or at least weekly is most useful), a manager can understand if the amount of time he or she planned for the work is going forward as envisioned. Knowing this earlier rather than later means the manager can

- Uncover performance flaws in the team and hopefully rectify the situation
- Question why the work isn't being done as planned, often uncovering the need for a change order to the client
- Reduce the time allotted in later phases of work if possible, to make up for increased time consumption in earlier phases
- Request additional time from the client

Involve the Client

Because any schedule is bound to change, a project manager should notify the client that the schedule may need to undergo alterations. If the client knows this upfront, designers have a much better chance of managing the client's expectations and heading off trouble and misunderstandings.

Planning and scheduling design is about forecasting. It's about making educated guesses and watching how these guesses play out in reality. Time management analysis—at the onset and throughout the project—is critical. A great project manager will look at the facts, such as time sheets and the completed work, and extrapolate out toward the final goal. Close observation of how the team is spending their time will allow the project manager to make better scheduling decisions in the future. Plus, a manager may be able to adjust the schedule for the current project by renegotiating with the client.

Scheduling Software

Project management software usually contains a scheduling component. These are often robust, and sometimes too labor intensive for the needs of many design projects. One great aspect of using this software is that it typically is linked to email. This is useful for alerting the manager or team members with built-in warnings about how much time has been used to date. Some designers simply use a web-based shared calendar as their project scheduling device. Others like project status reports that are essentially daily to-do lists emailed to the team. Still others have quick daily face-to-face team meetings to review the previous day's work and chart the course for that day's activities. Use whatever level of complexity and detail your team prefers.

Software Shows What Takes Precedence

Nearly every design firm will benefit from someone looking at the firm's overall work flow and capacity. A manager needs to look at any potentially conflicting due dates and client demands. One of the best ways to facilitate this is to use scheduling software.

The relationship between and among the different activities required to complete a project that must be done in a particular sequence is called a precedence relationship. Software is a good means for tracking and managing these relationships. A map of the tasks that must be completed before the next step is begun can easily be visualized in a Gantt chart (see page 69), which many scheduling software programs create.

Software Helps Contingency Planning

Design managers may wish to build in some extra time to complete a task or phase of work, by indicating on the schedule that the work will take longer than they know it will. This is called contingency planning. Building in time contingency, and then managing to that time frame, will help the team stay on schedule. For example, if an activity is slated to be done on Thursday, ask for the work at the end of the day Wednesday to ensure that the work is completed for Thursday. Allowing some slack in a schedule means a manager has a little bit of a buffer, and understands precisely how much a schedule can slip before it causes real delays and problems for the project.

One caveat: Giving false due dates and then sitting on the work or making arbitrary additional changes to it because you have the time will annoy the design team and undermine your credibility.

Triage and the Design Firm

Since most design firms are small businesses, they must constantly be juggling resources. Often, the same personnel need to work on a variety of projects simultaneously. Design projects are not always in an active state—designers often must stop what they're doing to wait for client approvals, content from collaborators, or manufacturing from suppliers. Issues and gaps can arise in any schedule that can cause the work at a design firm to come to a halt. It just makes good business sense for the design firm to fill in those gaps with other work.

Coordinating the requirements of several simultaneous projects can be complicated for a design firm. It requires a kind of 3-D thinking: monitoring what is happening, tracking expectations, and anticipating next steps.

So that no client or project suffers, someone has to keep track of all open jobs, much like a triage nurse sorts patients in a hospital emergency room according to urgency. To make triage decisions and juggle project demands, ask yourself
- What must we absolutely get done?
- How does the work look after it's slotted into day-parts (morning, afternoon, evening)?
- What can slide until the next day?
- Which jobs now require a change in schedule?
- Who has to be alerted of this change in schedule?
- How does this change affect the overall delivery dates for each open job in the firm?
- Who are we disappointing?
- What is the financial value of that disappointed client to our firm's business? Should we be disappointing them—or some other client?
- What are the repercussions, if any, of a missed deadline?

Case Study in Planning:

Lorenc + Yoo Design / Atlanta, Georgia USA

Lorenc + Yoo Design's reputation is built around versatility, rather than a signature style. Partners Jan Lorenc and Chung Youl Yoo lead their environmental communication design firm from the perspective of telling brand stories in physical surroundings. Their work includes signage, sculpture, retail space, furniture, and exhibition design for an international client base. The planning involved in work of this complexity and scale is apparent in viewing it. "My role is to serve primarily as the design director, setting the tone and handling the upfront research and spirit of the project," explains Lorenc. "Chung primarily handles the evolution of bringing the design idea into reality, negotiating with the manufacturers, detailing the individual pieces of the project, and selecting the final finishes and materials." With their staff, they sometimes work for years to bring concepts to reality.

UPS

Calm, sophisticated, and with an understated Chinese feel, the 4,000 square foot (372 m²) space for UPS's presence at the 2008 Summer Olympic Games features four distinct areas: two dining rooms, a lounge area, and a bar. It became a home away from home for UPS guests, a place of refuge from the hustle and bustle of the games. Tipping a hat to UPS's brand message and slogan, "What can brown do for you?" the space's dominant color is brown. However, the design firm accented each area with yellows, gold, and greens to communicate modernity and a blending of aesthetics from the East and the West.

Briefing documents summarized the design rationale and explain Lorenc + Yoo Design's strategy and themes. Because this was a hospitality suite at the Olympics, the environment needed to capture a sense of place and the excitement of the games, and celebrate achievement while being a refuge of quiet comfort in Beijing. Design motifs juxtapose both ancient and modern Chinese cultural icons.

Echoing the message of openness and global opportunity delivered by UPS, there is no place where guests feel closed off from the other areas. The design team achieved this by

designing "moon gates" (below, middle) that acted as windows throughout the space. Inspired by Asian garden elements in which gates are used to frame a particular plant or vista with a round opening.

The ideas revolved around a celebration of Chinese ethos and mystery, while playing off the vibrancy, hustle, and energy of modern China. "We wanted to create a sense of a journey," says Lorenc, "that invites guests of the games to enjoy a sense of international travel and adventure, and leaves them with memories that will last a lifetime."

As seen in these images, abundant narrative possibilities are evident in the exhibit's 3-D applications and the companion collateral used throughout the UPS suite. Design and written communications draw from metaphors and allegories in Western–Far Asian history, including ancient seafarers, traders, and epic historic events and cultural icons. Elements and inspiration came from many sources, including the Forbidden City, the Great Wall, and even modern Beijing.

"Lorenc +Yoo Design has a holistic approach, an integrated, seamless design philosophy, and is driven by a mission to tell clients' stories, not its own. This is visible in our work for UPS at the 2008 Olympics."
—Jan Lorenc, partner,
Lorenc+Yoo Design

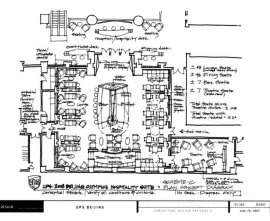

Case Study in Planning:

Lorenc + Yoo Design / Atlanta, Georgia USA

Il Milano

Lorenc + Yoo was hired to design canopies for a fifteen-year-old building designed by Philip Johnson in downtown Atlanta. The 191 Tower is a fifty-five-story corporate office building that houses the regional headquarters for Deloitte. The building has a cathedral-like appearance, and at the time bore little or no identification of the tenants inside. The firm designed a series of canopies that allows for building identification as well as that of its major anchors, including the restaurant Il Mulino. Lorenc + Yoo studied the context of the building—its scale, color, and classical design—for inspiration.

BELOW

There are three canopies: one central hanging canopy that measures 33 × 12 × 5 ft. (10.1 × 3.7 × 1.5 m); one restaurant canopy on the left side for Il Mulino restaurant that measures 17 × 8 × 4 ft. (5.2 × 2.4 × 1.2 m); and one amenity directory sign on the left that measures 17 × 4 × 9 ft. (5.2 × 1.2 × 2.7 m). The canopies are constructed of green frosted glass with gold accents. The central canopy bears a golden emblem of the 191 Building, while the others feature Art Deco-era typography.

Greektown

When Greektown Casino decided to expand and build a new hotel tower, its architects, Hnedak Bobo Group, recommended that it hire Lorenc + Yoo to design the signage. The new wayfinding system is both functional and aesthetically tied in with the architecture.

BELOW, LEFT

The exterior signage reflects the original signs, some of which are still in place, but with a modern twist. Whereas the old signs used individual bulbs (think Broadway marquis signs), the new ones use LEDs. The overall feel of the signs is the same, and they use the full five-color palette of the Greektown logo in both paint and neon.

BELOW

The interior casino signs relied heavily on Greek themes, using patterns and colors found in the casino. In the hotel, however, the treatment is more refined, paying homage to the wonderful interior designed by the architecture firm Rossetti. Prismatic gold letters mounted directly to dark wood walls lend an air of distinction.

Case Study in Planning:

Lorenc + Yoo Design / Atlanta, Georgia USA

Samsung

Samsung Electronics, a global leader in mobile phones, decided to step away from traditional billboards in favor of a more artistic approach to advertising. In January 2010, Samsung unveiled its newest mobile phone model atop a Lorenc + Yoo-designed, aluminum sculpture of a hand at the Frankfurt Airport in Germany. Similar structures were unveiled at airports in the Ukraine, Toronto, and other global locations.

Called *Rising Hand*, the polished-aluminum sculpture with baked-on red acrylic rises 50 feet (15.2 m). It features a hand holding a Samsung mobile phone. The sculpture has a powerful upward thrust that is futuristic and dynamic.

Curving toward the sky to symbolize the limitless possibilities in the future of communication, the sculpture embodies Samsung's philosophy of "The World in Your Hand." Lorenc + Yoo based the hand on a traditional Greek column but reduced it to its basic anatomical

elements: narrowing as it rises, and culminating with a grasping hand holding a mobile phone that is a sort of key to the world.

Sketches below show the project's evolution. "We like to show scrawls, notes, study models, computer models, spatial videos, and computer interactives," says Lorenc. The firm uses these items in each phase of project planning and execution. They tell the story of the team members' interaction with each other and their client. Rather than creating a realistic hand, Lorenc + Yoo

created a modern abstract form that suggests energy, triumph, and the power of global communications. The silver color of the sculpture echoes its technological roots, while red accents convey the energy and human spirit of the hand.

"The key to effective exhibition design lies not only in an ability to balance utility and aesthetics but also in an awareness of contextual and historical relevance. This process requires a keen awareness of the client's objective: Our passion is to express the client's passion. Colors, materials, typography, lighting, and other details must all work together so that the environment is seamless... We use environments to send messages in useful and beautiful ways."
—Jan Lorenc, design director, Lorenc + Yoo

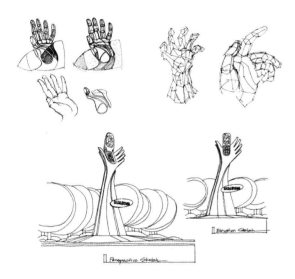

Design Process: Storytelling through Space
By Jan Lorenc

Our work is typically coordinated with a team of architects, interior designers, landscape architects, content developers, client liaisons and marketing professionals who work both inside and outside the firm. The basis of our team's creative process is a holistic investigation into the organization or the story in need of communication. This method uncovers the client's individual story and expresses it in a coherent and attractive manner. Our approach looks at the company or environment and strives to incorporate the richness of its culture and context into the project. Everything from the site plan to the landscape, lighting, building interiors and graphic images down to the micro level is part of the unified and unique narrative.

Multidisciplinary collaboration creates rich visual and program designs by engaging clients' various constituents—donors, scientists, teachers and other community members—and by developing stakeholder involvement and participation. This helps to make complex stories and subject matter accessible to children, visitors, employees, or donors and cultivates community stakeholders to ensure the longevity of the project.

Our design process is drawing intensive and uses multiple analysis and documentation approaches. This ensures that all project stakeholders are fully engaged and contribute to the unified story. A project may include storyboards, a design element matrix, a planning analysis, and a written narrative. We also focus on integrating dynamic technology into our storytelling. Rich interactive environments are the most effective in telling ongoing, evolving stories. Dynamic media is integrated into nearly every exhibition, with content management being an integral part of the design process.

As individual design specialists add their expertise, the client's story becomes more refined and developed. Despite the high level of collaboration, the project designer maintains the leading role, making sure that the message is consistently articulated from top to bottom.

Ten Reasons Design Project Schedules Fail

Every design project brings its own unique challenges.
Here are some common reasons why design projects to go off track:

1 Creativity means uncertain durations—it doesn't always happen exactly within a specific time allotment

2 Problems on another project demand the team's attention and everyone must focus on addressing that and not the current project

3 Client delays in approval or providing information

4 A poorly forecasted or overly optimistic schedule was created by the project manager

5 Technological troubles— software conflicts, IT issues, bad file management

6 Steeper learning curve than anticipated

7 More client and/or designer revisions were required, causing more work and expanding time requirements as well

8 Bad creative brief, meaning poorly defined scope of work, incorrect Work Breakdown Structure, resourcing, and scheduling. Essentially, working on the wrong problem in the wrong way and wasting time.

9 Unforeseen complexity and degree of difficulty

10 Poor communication and team interaction

Details, Details, Details: Asset Management

Planning is a multitiered exercise. Trying to conceive of every possible contingency in a design project is an exercise in futility. It's best to just review the major issues, forecast as much as possible, and adapt as the project moves from point A to point Z. So many things can go wrong in a design project, and most of them concern missed details—those hundreds of little things that must be factored in, remembered, and utilized to develop great design. Doing the job right means getting those details right.

From the beginning, you must set up a means of communication and sharing creative assets. An asset is any file, physical object, element, or artifact that is created or utilized for a design project. Asset management is not strictly a planning issue, but you must plan a work flow method among designers that supports good collaboration. If you've ever seen a design team's work stopped or delayed because they printed out the wrong version of a file or they must revise finished art because they used the wrong version of the client's logo, you've seen the problems inherent in not managing the details and assets of a job properly. These issues can cost significant time and money.

Good File Hygiene

Because nearly all of the designers' work product—whether in progress or finished—is digital, creating a basic digital asset management system is fast and relatively easy. However, it takes some time and a lot of commitment to maintain the system on an ongoing basis. Here are the rules for using a bare-bones digital asset management system:

- Use unique job numbers for each project (see page 51).
- Set up a folder for each client.
- Within the client folder, place folders for each unique job number.
- Within each numbered job folder, create a subfolder called:
  - **RESEARCH** (all background information)
  - **IMAGES** (all illustrations, photography, and logos to be used in the work)
  - **STUDIES** (all work in progress)
  - **PRESENTATIONS** (all client presentations and PDFs)
  - **FINALS** (all finished art)
  - **COPY** (all copy and text to be used in the job)
- Name each document in all of these files consistently with a date and job number code; for example, 01_02_10_ABC101

If everyone on the design team understands the naming and filing conventions—whether it is the system suggested here or something else—and complies with it, the project's assets will be easy to find and use. The result is a consistently and properly managed scheme for good file hygiene that will reduce time consumption, improve work flow, cut down on errors, help avoid duplication of effort especially because of lost items, boost collaborative sharing, and promote efficiency, all of which will improve responsiveness, speed up the work, and reduce costs.

A variety of software solutions—web-based and internal network—aid in digital asset management. They involve tagging the files with metadata (e.g., client information, file type, categories, graphic elements, classification, media, designer name, version codes, etc.) and can be expensive and time-consuming to administer. But in large organizations with many users, multiple projects, and, especially, various branches, it is worth the time and effort to implement one of these systems.

Project Profile in Planning:
Garaz designed by Siedemzero / Warsaw, Poland

Garaz

Garaz #3 features skateboard culture–inspired music and video. Siedemzero designed the DVD packaging and promotional collateral, including the movie's one sheet poster. The graphics are witty, bold, and rough around the edges.

"The fact that I live in Poland obviously has a significant effect on my work. It may seem odd, but I come from a generation that was raised during the time when Poland was a very empty place. All the things people dreamed about practically did not exist. The only thing left was self-initiative."
—Pawel Piotr Przybl, creative director, Siedemzero

Benchmarking

Because graphic design is an iterative and collaborative process, logical points, benchmarks, or milestones occur during the course of work and present themselves at the end of phases (see the process chart on pages 10–11 for more information about phases of work).

In business, the word *benchmark* suggests certain standards being met. In design, it typically is used to mean a phase deadline for completion of a certain amount of work. If we merge the two meanings and look at benchmarking in planning as finishing the work to a particular standard of expectation, benchmarking becomes a holistic tool for monitoring the design process.

Graphic Design Benchmarks

Here are some common design project benchmarks:
- Kickoff meeting
- Creative brief
- Design criteria
- Design strategy
- First presentation of design
- Design refinements
- Approval of final design
- Release of finished artwork files

What Impacts Benchmarks?

When looking at how well the design team is meeting their goals and benchmarks, review the following items, as they impact the success of benchmarks:

▶ **Creative Leadership**

Having a clear vision, understanding and providing feedback based on a creative brief, and coaching and mentoring the design team to get the best creative out of them. Typically, this is the creative director's job, but it also is heavily affected by the client.

▶ **Rigorous Culture**

Having an environment where deadlines are respected, work flow is orderly, and yet creative excellence is also revered. For both business and design, creative excellence is a result of a vigorous culture.

▶ **Skilled Personnel**

Not just having enough people, but the right people, working together on the project. Each person has definite roles and responsibilities. These people must possess creative muscle and know how to use it.

▶ **Proper Motivation**

Having a love for the challenge of solving problems and utilizing talent. There probably are lazy designers in the world, but most designers are intensely motivated to do great work, and they genuinely enjoy the design process. Designers who don't feel this way probably are in the wrong profession.

Bigger Questions

To assess benchmarks, a manager needs some specific measurable areas of performance to determine how well the project is progressing. This can be as simple as seeing if the project's interim deadline was completed as scheduled. Don't just ask: Is it done? Instead, ask: How well is it done? Does it meet our expectations? Will it meet the client's expectations? It can also be as complex as assessing the job performance of certain designers to see if they are meeting expectations on the project.

So much of design and the design process is subjective. The more objective metrics that can be employed, the more designers can repeat their successes. At the end of the day, however, it comes down to client satisfaction and design effectiveness. Here, too, graphic design is often evaluated on objective criteria. It is worth our efforts as an industry to have a measurable process with clear benchmarks that can be communicated and that can prove design's value to business. The incremental steps carefully monitored and recorded by a project manager become evidence of a professional measurable methodology that improves the client's ROI (return on investment).

Chapter 4
Budgeting

Budgeting for Design

A lot of designers think money is a main reason they win or lose a client's business. They are often right. Pricing work properly is a skill acquired through practice. It takes a keen instinct for what the marketplace will pay and what the design firm will need.

How the work is priced is only one factor in getting a design job from a client. Other factors from the client's perspective include

- **Relevant Experience**
  Has the designer worked on a similar project in the past? What does it look like? What are the results of the design?
- **Right Attitude**
  Is the designer enthusiastic and eager to begin work on the project?
- **Good Chemistry**
  Does it seem like a good fit? Does the designer "get us"? Do we like the designer as a person?
- **Portfolio/Style**
  Is the designer's work appealing? Does it have a discernible style that meshes with our needs? Is the designer creative enough?
- **Perceived Reliability**
  Did the designer show up on time? Do we think we can trust the designer? (Since the client is sometimes meeting the designer for the first time, this is often subjective.)
- **A Referral**
  Did someone we know and trust refer this designer to us? Did the designer get a good recommendation?
- **Luck**
  Is the designer in the right place at the right time?

It is arguable which comes first—creating a schedule or creating a budget. Sometimes a client just tells the designer how much money they have for a particular project. Usually, though, the client requests a price from the designer. The designer's compensation is an essential element in a designer–client agreement.

Pricing is what you tell the client it will cost for the project. This includes fees (your compensation) and expenses (reimbursable outside costs for items purchased for the project). Budgeting is how you appropriate and manage these fees and expenses. In this chapter, we'll look at money in both ways.

Here are some key factors to consider when pricing a design job:

- **Scope of Work**
  What exactly are we doing? What services are we providing? What are the deliverables? In what format?
- **Resources**
  Who will do the work? Do we have to supplement our team with additional designers? With what skills? How much do they cost? Do we need our senior or junior designers to do the work?
- **Scheduling**
  How much time do we have? How much time do we need? How much time does each team member need? Do we need to juggle several projects simultaneously? How does that affect us?
- **The Client**
  Have we worked for this client before? Are they decisive or prone to revisions? Are there layers of management that must be appeased or is there one decision maker? How available is that person?
- **Collaborators**
  Beyond designers, who else needs to work on this project? What will they do? What will it cost? How much will be provided directly by the client?
- **Quality**
  What are the client's expectations? Are they willing to pay for it? Have we done something like this before? Will there be a lot of research, or can we immediately get to work?
- **Expertise**
  Do we have it? How steep is the learning curve if we don't? How will we know when we have a great design for this client?
- **Cash Flow**
  What other jobs are in-house right now? How much money do we need? Design is a business, and all businesses have real financial requirements and obligations. What are ours?

The answers to these questions have cost implications. The more experienced a design manager is at answering and anticipating these tough questions and the better his or her documented records are on previous projects, the more accurate the design manager will be in pricing and budgeting projects.

Pricing Factors

It keeps coming back to time and money. A design firm has only so many hours per week to sell. For many firms, pricing the work comes down to

Hourly Rate
× Estimated Hours
Required
―――――――――
= Project Fee

Of course, straight time is not the only factor in establishing a design fee. Here's what else to consider:

- Expertise in this area: Are we the leaders in this category of design? What is our track record? Can we charge a premium because of that?
- Historical records: What have we charged for similar jobs in the past? What will the market bear?
- Value of the work: It's subjective, but what will the market bear? What do you think this client will pay?
- Page rate: This is a per-page fee that's good for publications or print websites based on estimated time or perhaps what you've charged another client.
- Client's stated budget: Sometimes, the client will tell the designer exactly what they are willing to pay. Believe them.
- Serendipity: What does your gut say? Or maybe, what kind of income do we need now?

Considering all of these things together will provide a well-rounded exploration of what the price should be. Losses on a particular job due to incorrect pricing can be absorbed, but a constant stream of work that is priced improperly, with the designer losing money or barely breaking even, will ultimately affect the firm's financial stability. Watching and continuing to learn in this area of design project management is critical.

Determine Your Rate

You can determine an hourly rate for design services in several ways. Many design organizations worldwide have published this kind of information as a reference. For example, in the United States, the AIGA publishes an annual wage and salary survey. You can divide the average annual salary reported in the survey by the number of billable hours in a year (1,500 hours is a good round-number average to use). This calculation gives you an hourly rate based on the organization's member submission information. A discussion with peers and colleagues may yield a ballpark idea of what they charge per hour. However, many people shy away from this kind of conversation and often don't tell the truth. If they trust you, and don't directly compete with you for client business, they may reveal this information.

Calculation Based on Real Needs

Here is a formula for determining your hourly rate based on your actual costs of staying in business. It's not the only way to determine an hourly rate, and it doesn't factor in the value of the work to a client's business or a premium for your expertise; it's merely based on actual economic needs.

1

Total your monthly expenses.
If you are a freelancer, include all your expenses from rent to food to entertainment. Design firms should include all overhead and labor (employee salaries and employee-related benefit costs). This total is your operating cost.

Monthly Expenses = X (Operating Costs)

2

Total your billable hours.
What are the total hours you have to sell in a month? A standard figure is eight hours per day, or forty hours per week, or 160 hours per month.

Total Billable Hours = 160 per month

Most designers don't bill all the hours of their day. On average, about 10 percent to 30 percent of their day is taken up with nonclient-billable activities, such as running the business, doing office-related tasks, or simply downtime. Therefore, to bill forty hours per week, you may need to work forty-four to fifty-four hours during that week.

3

Get your break-even rate.
Divide your monthly expenses by your monthly billable hours. The result is the hourly break-even rate you must achieve to pay your monthly expenses.

X (Operating Costs) ÷ by 160 monthly hours = Break-Even Hourly Rate

4

Determine your published rate.
To build in profit and savings, and set aside some money for income taxes, you'll need to add money to increase your break-even hourly rate. Multiply your break-even rate by three for a number that can be called your published rate. That is the rate you give your clients, and you use to calculate your fixed project fees. If you charge your clients on an hourly basis rather than a fixed project fee, use this rate. Also use the published rate to calculate any additional compensation on change orders (see page 40).

Break-Even Hourly Rate × 3 = Published Hourly Rate

Why multiple by a factor of three? Because one-third is your income, one-third is for taxes, and one-third should be split in half for profit and for savings to reinvest into the business for emergencies, research and development, or self-promotion. Using thirds works well for taxes in the United States. Other countries may have other tax ratios and designers should consider those when determining their published hourly rate.

Profit and Hourly Rates
Instead of implementing step 4, as described, some designers add a percentage for profit or contingencies into their monthly overhead expenses when calculating their operating costs. Step 4 simply provides an easy way to determine an hourly rate that factors everything in.

Reviewing Pricing

Designers must know their hourly rate to set their fee for particular design jobs—both the breakeven hourly rate to understand the lowest fee they should charge, and the published hourly rate to allow for profit and tax obligations (see page 95). Calculating a fee using both sets of rates shows you where the job must be priced (breakeven) and what is an optimum price (published hourly rate). However, it is hard to know exactly how many hours it will take to do any design project. Therefore, any estimate based on hours is just that: an educated guess on the duration and complexity of the work. As such, pricing jobs strictly on hourly rates is not a 100 percent accurate approach.

Evaluating Your Calculations

To get a more well-rounded view of pricing, review the project total you calculated using your published hourly rate and ask yourself the following questions:

Does this total reflect the value of this work to the client? Does it reflect the expertise we bring to the project?

Can we get more money for this job based on who the client is? In other words, is this client a small regional startup company or a well-funded multinational corporation? Little businesses typically have little budget, and big businesses should have a big budget. What have we charged for similar projects in the past? How is this project the same or different from those? Is that reflected in this price calculation?

What do we think our competitors would charge for this project? Why do we think that? Can we discuss our calculation with anyone?

(Talking about pricing design with a colleague or two is fine. Note, however, that in most countries, banding together as a profession and determining an industrywide price is illegal. It's a form of collusion called price-fixing. This is why design organizations as a group rarely discuss in public or publish pricing information.)

Is there any published information on pricing for this type of work? For example, the *Graphic Artist Guild's Pricing and Ethical Guidelines* publishes rate information. The organization polls its members, has them price certain kinds of projects, and then publishes that information. It can legally do this in the United States because it is a trade union, and it operates under different laws than nonprofit design (arts) organizations.

Does this price calculation seem high or low based on your gut instinct? How should it be adjusted?

Learning about Pricing

Two design firms can have the same published hourly rate and calculate two different project fees using that rate. For example, one design firm may work slower or have more people involved; this means it estimates more hours into a project and it charges more. Only by keeping very good records, especially time sheets, on all projects and then comparing estimates to actual costs can designers price their work accurately over time.

A trusted client may be candid and tell the designer what competitors would charge on a particular job, particularly if the designer lost the job to a competitor. It's important to learn why a design firm lost out on an opportunity, but remember that it isn't always a question of money.

Another useful strategy is to develop relationships with other designers that can include discussions of money.

Remember that big fees don't necessarily mean big profits. It all comes down to how the project is run. How long did the designer work on the project to earn that fee? Maybe we spent very little time on the project, but the work was tremendously valuable to the client's business. These things are unique to every design project. It is why most designers are always wondering whether they charged enough on a job and whether they could have made more money.

Money Categories for Pricing

All estimated design projects must include the following categories of money:

1. Fees

A designer's compensation for a particular project. It is a common graphic design industry standard to bill the fee as estimated, handling it as a fixed or set fee, no matter what occurs during the project which might alter the time/value/money ratio. The exception to this rule is when the project deviates from the designer–client agreement, and a change order has been submitted and approved. In that way, the fee may be increased.

2. Expenses

These are all of the reimbursable out-of-pocket costs for items purchased specifically for the project (not overhead costs). It is a common graphic design industry standard to add a markup or service charge on all expenses of 15 percent to 25 percent. Justification for this charge includes
- The fact that a designer guarantees the quality and timely delivery of the item purchased.
- It is a convenience to the client to have the designer purchase the item.
- The designer typically buys the item and then waits to bill the client for it, therefore acting as a temporary loan of sorts.

Primarily however, designers add a markup because it is an industry-standard practice in the profession. Whatever your practice in regard to markups and service charges, just make sure it is clear in the designer–client agreement. Keep it all above board and you won't run into any problems.

Project Profile in Budgeting:

Old Republic designed by Larsen / Minneapolis, Minnesota, and San Francisco, California USA

Old Republic Title Company

Tim Larsen founded Larsen in 1975 with a desire to stand for graphic design excellence—in the work his firm produced, the people he collaborated with, and the results he achieved. Three decades later, Larsen has built an international client list, attracted some of the best creative talent in the industry, and created award-winning branding, interactive, print, and environmental graphics work. Larsen has produced work for more than 140 clients worldwide, from entrepreneurial startups to Fortune 100s, across a variety of industries.

Since 1997, Old Republic Title has partnered with Larsen to design its annual report. By listening to the client and developing an understanding of the insurance business, Larsen has established a high level of service and expectation. The company appreciates how Larsen's creative solutions tell the story the insurer wants to share. Through visually stunning design, attention-grabbing concepts, and direct messages, Old Republic Title's annuals acknowledge challenges and demonstrate economic optimism and stability. Year after year, this consistent brand attitude conveys trust and wins devotion for the company. With their elegant design and engaging copy, the annual reports also serve as excellent marketing pieces, appealing to real estate agents, loan processors, lenders, and attorneys.

Why is title insurance important? That's the simple but powerful question Old Republic Title posed in its annual report. Larsen's use of rich photography and targeted messaging provides the evocative answer: "It protects what matters most." Through this theme, Larsen helped Old Republic Title command the attention of key audiences with colorful, penetrating photographs of the people it serves, paired with compelling headlines.

Simplicity, flexibility, strength, and comprehensiveness: How to say it all in a way that makes customers act? Keen for the challenge, Larsen created a series of visually intriguing images for Old Republic Title with the theme "Good Things Come in ____ Packages." Each image attempts to package the intangible by filling in the blank and using ironic and imaginative line drawings combined with photographs of typical Old Republic Title clients.

It may be easy to take title insurance for granted, but imagine losing a home or business. Without the right title insurance coverage, it's a very real possibility. "Because you have a lot to lose" addresses this issue with a unique combination of original photography and illustration. The bright color palette reinforces the positive benefits of choosing Old Republic Title.

The copy-driven approach to this annual report showed how quickly little errors can confuse something as simple as a headline—or as complex as a property title. The report's flawed headline is edited error by error over four introductory spreads, depicting how Old Republic Title finds and corrects errors on the titles it insures. Energetic colors demonstrate the firm's vitality, and the report's sign-off—"We do good deeds"—simply and effectively restates the value proposition.

The year 2006 was tough for many title insurance companies, but unlike its competitors, Old Republic Title saw plenty of reasons to be optimistic about the future. Larsen captured and communicated that confidence in "Looking Up." Affirmative front-of-book copy and an engaging blend of original photography and illustrated stars were combined in a welcoming booklet format.

In the midst of the real estate crisis, Old Republic Title wanted to convey strength and confidence. The metaphor of a door—a real estate icon—symbolizes "opening the door to opportunity." Intense primary colors provide a sense of optimism and hope while custom illustrations and playful die-cut pages emphasize the door concept, revealing a new benefit to working with Old Republic on every page.

"As designers, we have the skill and responsibility to help others make good choices about the marks they leave on the world."
—Tim Larsen, president
and founder, Larsen

"You're mad as heck," states the opening page of the annual report, referencing a year of economic challenges. An attention-grabbing cover presents a seemingly profane statement, !$#@%, which the report's interior cleverly breaks down into individual messages of positive news. Constituents discover they aren't alone in their frustration, and that despite a constant stream of negative news from everyone else, Old Republic Title still has good news to share.

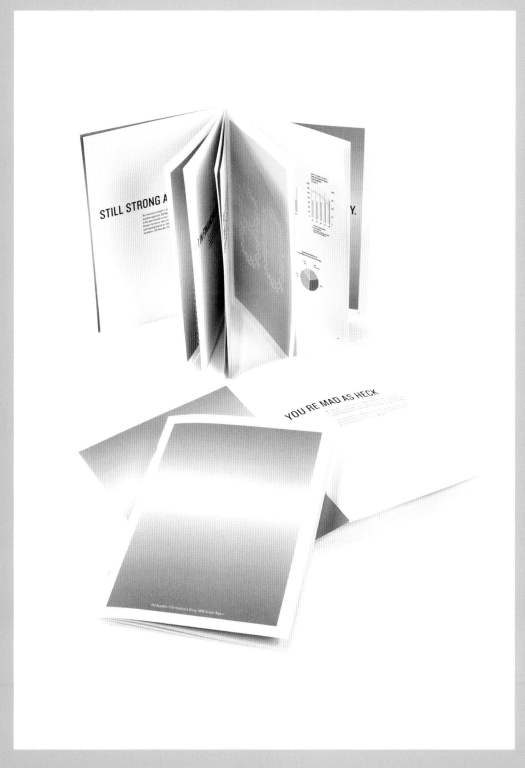

Breaking Down a Budget

When thinking about pricing a project, it's logical to consider who will be doing the work. The members of a design firm are likely paid at different rates depending on experience and expertise. For example, a partner in the firm will typically have a higher rate than a junior designer. Therefore, in calculating a fee, consider what it costs the firm to do the work. If a junior designer is doing 75 percent of the work, the project can be priced lower. Alternatively, you can calculate the price by determining the average rate of all the designers in the firm. This is called a blended hourly rate or collective hourly rate.

Individual versus Collective or Blended Rates

Many design firms utilize their blended hourly rate when creating their published hourly rate. Often, they do this because in many projects, everyone on the staff is involved at some point, so rather than trying to determine the exact number of hours each person will spend on the project, the manager estimates the total number of hours the job will require. For some designers, this calculation is simply easier.

If the firm uses design project management software, it will be prompted to identify an hourly rate for an individual (presumably based on salary and benefit costs) and for particular tasks (e.g., strategy is more expensive than production of finished files). With these computer programs, it's easy to look at project costs from several different angles, which is always a good practice in pricing graphic design.

Pricing versus Budgeting

Pricing a job is, in essence, estimating: getting an overall sense of the fees and expenses a design project requires. These are the money numbers that go into a designer–client agreement. Budgeting a job is about allotting specific amounts of time and money, based on the approved fees and expenses in the designer–client agreement, for specific tasks that occur in the working of a project. Admittedly, these are somewhat arbitrary definitions of the terms. The view taken in this book is that they are related but different ways of thinking about design projects and money.

For budgeting, let the work breakdown structure (page 66) be the road map. Assign one person to each task, and identify the amount of time you think it will take to complete the task. When the job commences, make sure the person performing each task knows how many hours have been planned for the work. The person should alert the manager about any impediment to following this plan as soon as it occurs. With that knowledge, the manager has options: Extend the schedule, provide extra support, or even present the client with a change order, depending on the cause of the impediment.

There is a complex relationship between the project constraints of time, cost, and scope (see page 15) and reviewing budgets. It's always about juggling opposing constraints and making the best decisions possible. For example, if the budget allocates three hours for completing design concepts, but nothing good has been created in that period, the designer must recalculate the budget to spend more time to develop a great design solution.

Attitudes About Money

Budgeting in design is another form of planning; an educated guess at a project's financial implications. Real-world circumstances sometimes turn these plans upside down. No designer can anticipate every possible factor that may compromise a budget, but designers can understand their own work ethic and philosophical approach to money that may aid or subvert their budgets.

Budget Worksheet

A budget worksheet can help you to visualize your budgets and determine how your fees and expenses will be managed. To use it, multiply each task in each phase of work by a task rate, an individual's published hourly rate, or the firm's average blended rate. (Remember to include fees from any subcontractors working on the project.) This is how designers can translate rates into fees.

Here's a budget worksheet mockup for the initial phases of a logo design project.

BUDGET WORKSHEET

Date: _____ Job #: _____
Client: _____
Project: _____

Phase 1: Orientation

In-House Services

Activity	Person	Hours		Rate		Total
Kickoff Meeting	_____	_____	x	_____	=	_____
Market Research	_____	_____	x	_____	=	_____
Design Research	_____	_____	x	_____	=	_____

Subcontracted Services

Activity	Person	Hours		Rate		Total
Kickoff Meeting	_____	_____	x	_____	=	_____
Market Research	_____	_____	x	_____	=	_____

Estimated Expenses

Item	Estimated Cost		Markup		Total
Color Printouts	_____	+	_____	=	_____
Travel	_____	+	_____	=	_____
Hotel/Meals	_____	+	_____	=	_____
Misc. Supplies	_____	+	_____	=	_____

Total Fees	=	_____
Total Expenses	=	_____
Budget Grand Total	=	_____

Pricing Philosophy

Design firms generally are driven by three philosophical attitudes:

- Client Demand Driven:
  Whatever the client wants, they get. Responsiveness is key. Going the extra mile to please the client, which often means rounds of revisions, is fine. This designer believes service is king and financial rewards will come over the course of the client relationship, not necessarily via one project.

- Design Driven:
  Quality and creativity are at the forefront, not money. These designers work until they achieve excellence, even if they exceed their allotted time on the project. They believe that doing great work will bring more and better clients, and the money will simply follow.

- Financially Driven:
  Cash is king for these designers. They believe design is a for-profit business; if the client wants more changes or enhanced quality, they need to pay more for it. These designers believe there are always more clients and more projects, but a bird in the hand is worth more than speculation about the future.

Clients and Money

Not all designers are driven by money. Scores of designers are much more interested in the artistic than the financial aspects of design. However, all designers need money to survive.

Reframing financial negotiations with clients means designers must be fully engaged in an active conversation with the client. They need to be confident about their ability to use design to meet their client's business goals; believe in the value of their work; and be willing to ask for fair compensation. Money often coincides with issues of self-worth, so you must believe in yourself and your abilities as a designer before negotiating fees in order to achieve the best outcome financially and creatively.

Tips for Dealing with Clients About Money

- Be clear. What exactly does the price include?
- Define payment terms. When do you expect to be paid? Upon completion? Within thirty days?
- Stick to the fee. If you must raise the fee, explain the increase in a change order.
- State the number of revisions and stick to them. Note any exceptions or additions in a change order.
- Keep good records. Provide time sheets and expense receipts as a backup to your billing if the client requests it.
- Integrate the schedule with regular cost reviews. Review these frequently, and communicate any problems or issues. Alert the client. Make sure you capture all time (e.g., telephone consultation, travel time, etc.).
- Don't surprise the client. To get paid quickly, make your invoices match your estimates exactly.
- Keep fees consistent. Base fees on a rate the client understands. No fire sales, no discounts, no arbitrary changes in pricing structure.
- Get it in writing. Have anything related to money signed by the client, for legal reasons and to prompt a detailed conversation about money before any work gets underway.
- Get all related client paperwork and financial information. Get a purchase order number if it's required. Include a vendor number on your invoices if you were assigned one. Introduce yourself to the contact person in accounts payable.
- Stay in communication. Do this throughout the process, with the client contact and the accounting department, if necessary
- Consider incentives. This can be a discount for prompt or fast payment of invoices, or a late fee as a penalty for slow-paying clients.

Questions for Negotiating

Sometimes, a client can't afford your fee. The question is: what is actually happening? Investigate further:

- Will they ever be able to afford it or is it a temporary problem?
- Do they want to work with you?
- Can the scope to reduce deliverables be narrowed?
- Can they provide you with referrals?
- Will you get a great portfolio piece?
- Will you gain recognition, credibility, or some other benefit besides money?
- Is it worth taking the job?

Sometimes, you may wish to negotiate pricing. Naturally, it needs to be in your best interest to do so. Here are some questions to ask:

- Can we have longer to work on the project, perhaps fitting this job in between other work?
- Will the project challenge us creatively and open new doors?
- Can we do research and learn new skills that are marketable to other clients by doing this job?
- Will we have a chance to work with some exciting new collaborators in brand new ways?

These factors may be interesting enough to you to make it worth dropping your prices to get the job.

Talking Revisions

Communicating with clients about revisions is a huge part of managing client expectations regarding money. The best strategy is to be clear in the designer–client agreement about how many revisions are included. That way, the client understands the meaning of revision and round of revisions, and when they will start receiving additional charges because of those changes. For more information, see page 40–41.

Even with this clearly spelled out, many designers are unsure how to corral their client and alert them that they have exceeded the planned scope and revision allotment, for fear of losing the client. If the client has agreed to the terms in the designer–client agreement, it is okay to bill them. Just let them know what is happening in a professional manner.

Too often, designers are afraid to ask for additional compensation for additional work. This makes it harder for the industry to be treated fairly in this aspect of the business. When you practice without fair compensation, including receiving additional fees for additional work, you are hurting not only yourself, but all designers everywhere.

Designer Fault

Some designers hesitate to charge for revisions because they feel they caused the revisions. This may be true. An evaluation will reveal the cause(s) of a revision in a design project. If it is poor performance on the designer's part, the designer should not charge it to the client.

Three Types of Estimates

You can use three major types of estimates to communicate costs to clients:

Ballpark Estimate:

This is an initial rough estimate based on high-level client objectives, with a large margin for uncertainty. The deliverables, scope of work, and corresponding resource requirements may not be clear yet, so out of necessity, the estimate must allow for these things. Typically, a price range, rather than a fixed fee is stated.

Budgetary Estimate:

This is a more accurate view of project-related costs based on a much clearer scope of work. It is contingent on a fairly accurate view of the work to be done, which still may be in a state of flux. As such, conditions and parameters should be stated—for example, "This estimate is based on available information, and will be reviewed based on approved design concept."

Definitive Estimate:

This is a time-consuming and detailed estimate created once the full scope of work, final deliverables, and detailed work flow are known. A full work breakdown structure (see page 66) is completed, the project is scheduled, and the team is assembled before the estimate is prepared.

Eight Payment Strategies

Designers can be compensated for their work by way of a variety of payment methods. Clients and designers should negotiate a payment strategy that meets both of their needs. Here are some interesting options:

1. Fixed Fee

Agree to a total fee for the project. Invoice 50 percent before work begins and 50 percent upon completion. Bill expenses at the end of the project. This is a good strategy for smaller projects with clear deliverables.

2. Progress Payment

A project is broken down into sequential phases of work, with the fees and, possibly, expenses invoiced at the completion of each phase. Related to this is dividing an agreed-upon project fee into monthly installments. These progress payments are based on the calendar, and not the work completed, as is the case with the phased approach.

3. Modular

Divide a large project into smaller modules of work and bill them as separate jobs. This works well for related but not sequential work. For example, design a company's corporate identity in January, and then do the website in June.

4. Retainer

In this ongoing designer–client relationship, the designer agrees to a fixed fee, typically invoiced monthly, for a specific amount of work. This strategy is good for ongoing publications or clearly defined repetitive tasks—for example, developing a new top page for a website every week.

5. Hourly

In this open-ended agreement, the client pays the designer a fixed hourly rate for every hour worked on a project. Good recordkeeping is essential here. Some clients ask for a not-to-exceed ceiling on hours prior to commencement of work to stay within a certain budget.

6. Deferred

The designer and client negotiate a fee, but payment is deferred until a mutually agreed-upon date. This is somewhat risky for the designer, but good for a client with a startup business. Perhaps the fee negotiated is slightly higher than normal to offset the risk.

7. Profit Participation

The designer agrees to be paid a certain fee, typically lower than his or her standard practice, but in addition receives profit participation in the client's business. This ties design effectiveness to sales and business results and is another good strategy for startup clients or new products the designer is intricately involved in creating.

8. Trade

The designer is paid in-kind with client services or products instead of with money. Such barter agreements work if a clear value for the designer's work is established. Make sure the design is traded for the wholesale (not retail) value of the client's service or product.

Project Profile in Budgeting:

**Sun Microsystems designed by Fibonacci Design Group, LLC /
Los Angeles, California USA**

Sun Microsystems

To quantify the intangibles of computer technology company Sun Microsystems' culture, a visual language was developed and incorporated into an employee film. "The grammar of this language was built on the employee value proposition and positive team member experiences," explains Fibonacci Design Group Partner Greg Mann. "The campaign engaged and motivated the team to 'live the brand' and help shape the future of Sun Microsystems." The film focused on the strengths and beliefs already developed for Sun's brand expression with a healthy dose of irreverence and fun.

BELOW
Fibonacci began work with a thorough brief from Sun's senior director of Employee Communications and Communities, Terry McKenzie. The documents outlined brand attributes and values and defined goals for employee retention and recruitment.

The *I Have the Best Job at Sun* short film captured a genuine expression of Sun's competitive difference as seen through its employees' eyes. Top Sun executives used the video extensively at internal and external presentations. Screens from the video are shown below.

Fibonacci Design Group Talks Money

Greg Mann reveals some of the ways he and partner Sloane Mann think about money and pricing their design.

Q. How do you approach estimating a job?
A. We tend to think in terms of the value of the job. It's very possible to design, say, an identity that requires x hours of time. If it is a high-profile client, that same logo has greater value than it would for a start-up that's more of a mom-and-pop organization. That identity has the potential to generate far greater attention and revenue for the high-profile client. We tend to build proposals on project pricing, with specific parameters attached, and use the addendum of an hourly rate to help contain and focus the process. For instance, "proposal includes the presentation of five to seven concepts, with three to five rounds of edits. Additional exploration of concepts will be billed at $175/hour.

Q. What are three main things you think about in pricing design?
A. We've got more than three things, we consider

1. Have we worked with the client before, and do we know whether they require a great deal of hand-holding, or tend to trust/respect our design sense, making the process more efficient? We're fine with either, but the process in each case will be different.
2. What will be the usage/visibility of the end product?
3. Is this a client from whom we receive a regular stream of work, or is this a one-time engagement?
4. Are we actually going to be supplying more than just design in order to ensure the success of the project? For instance, will we be defining the marketing strategy for a client that is unable to do so for themselves?
5. How much do we love this project? Will it be an amazing experience or will it just be paying the bills?

Q. How do you know that you are charging a fee that is fair to the client and yourself?
A. We have, on occasion, asked a client for an honest assessment of comparable charges for projects that are specialized and within a given field. I think clients are often pleasantly surprised by this, and give honest, ethical answers (in part, because they know you are being mindful of their budgets). We have also asked fellow designers what they would charge for a project that we are bidding on, just to get a sense of where our numbers fall. We do, at times, also track hours on project priced design, just to make sure we are not falling below a minimum hourly rate.

Rights and Compensation

One thing designers must consider in terms of money and design is ownership of the work being created. Who owns what, and how the work may or may not be used, is a negotiating point that also has financial implications. This concept is tied to the designer's intellectual property rights and the client's right to use the work they commissioned the designer to create.

Intellectual property (a legal reference to the creations of the mind: inventions, literary and artistic works, etc.) is debated by lawyers worldwide. In the United States and Canada, for example, all creative work is owned by its creator until the creator transfers ownership in writing to someone else. This is the cornerstone of copyright protection (legal protection that gives the creator of an original work exclusive rights to use that work within a certain period). Other countries may take different views and have different laws, so designers must understand what is true and legal in the country in which they practice design.

There are some complex rights and usage agreements that can affect a graphic designer. For example, in the United States many clients require designers to work under a work-for-hire contract, which is a written (not verbal) legal agreement between the designer and client stating that the client owns all work developed by the designer under the contract. In essence, it legally makes the client the creator of the work and affords them all the related rights of a creator. This isn't a bad thing, but it means the client is now undisputedly the owner of the work. As such, a designer might want additional compensation.

It is important that the designer and client know who owns the work and how it may be used. For example, when a client owns outright an illustration that a designer developed for a pamphlet, the client can use that image in any future advertisement or on their web page, without paying the designer anything additional. Therefore, a designer would want to charge more for this kind of complete transfer of rights and ownership. Alternatively, it could be a negotiating point: Charge a lower fee, but the client has restricted usage rights for the work.

Compensation and the notion of intellectual property is a good topic for a designer to discuss with an attorney. You can also seek information from various design organizations, and share this information with your peers. Know your rights, know your client's needs, and know the laws at the intersection of these two things.

Factors to consider when thinking about the material worth of usage rights and your corresponding fee for a design include
- The value placed on similar work (perhaps even for other clients)
- The category or media in which the work will be used
- The geographic location or area of distribution for the work
- How the client will use the work (for what purpose)
- How long the work will be used
- How many items will be produced that incorporate the work

Licensing Options

Most of the work graphic designers do will be commissioned by a client for a mutually agreed upon sum or fixed project fee. However, some designers license their work to clients instead. Licensing means allowing or granting use of an original work for varied compensation based on the license. Usually, licensing takes one of these two forms in design:

Use-based Licensing

The designer's compensation is based on how the work is used.
- This often occurs for images such as illustration and photography.
- It's frequently negotiated for publications, print or digital.
- Additional uses, or changes in use, require additional agreements and compensation to the designer.
- Payment by the licensee (client) is typically made to the licensor (designer) before the work is used.

Royalty-based Licensing

The designer's compensation is a royalty or a percentage of the money received from the net sales of a product that incorporates the designer's work.
- This often occurs for merchandise for sale.
- It's frequently negotiated by product designers.
- Compensation is tied to sales and the public's acceptance of the product.
- The licensee (client) must allow the licensor (designer) to review accounting/product sales records.
- Payments typically are made quarterly, but can be negotiated otherwise.
- An advance on royalties is a payment the licensee (client) makes to the licensor (designer) upfront that is then deducted from the royalties to be paid in the future.

Even if you do not choose to be paid under a licensing agreement, your subcontractors may prefer to be paid this way. For example, it is common for an illustrator to allow his or her work to be utilized through a use-based licensing agreement.

Project Profile in Budgeting:

Honda designed by Wieden + Kennedy Tokyo / Tokyo, Japan

Honda: Drive Every Drop

Honda's Drive Every Drop campaign targets consumers in the Asia Oceania market. Created by Wieden + Kennedy Tokyo in conjunction with sister agency Wieden + Kennedy London, the campaign features print, web, and broadcast spots. The concept in the campaign is to get people to think about the amount of fuel used on their journeys—drop by drop, rather than gallon by gallon—and specifically to consider the environmental benefits of Honda's i-VTEC engine, which is designed to get the most out of every drop of fuel.

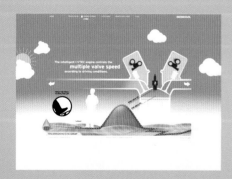

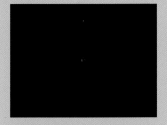

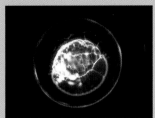

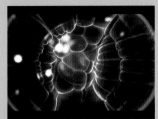

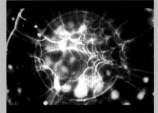

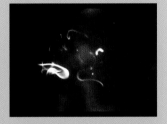

OPPOSITE
The Honda Drive Every Drop website leads users on three road trips:
from Delhi to Mumbai, from Kuala
Lumpur to Singapore, and from
Sydney to Tasmania. The site also
contains a set of TV commercials
and print advertisements, along
with an interactive, informative
introduction to the technology
behind the Honda i-VTEC engine.

ABOVE
Honda's i-VTEC engine is the result
of years of research and experimen-
tation, following the dream of developing an engine that consumes
less while keeping the power that
Honda engines are known for. It
is an intelligent VTEC system that
switches the valve timing for maximum efficiency during startup and
acceleration to achieve powerful
performance, and then delays intake
valve closure timing during cruising
and other low-load conditions for
improved fuel economy. The TV ads
spotlight these engine features.

How Weiden + Kennedy Tokyo Looks at Budgets

Q. Got any tips for talking to clients about money?
A. Budgets are always a challenging topic, even more so since
the economic downturn. Clients simply want more with less. They
are smarter and better informed about how new technologies can
work for them in both media and production techniques and how
these elements can extend their reach through more inexpensive
means. They are more cautious about how to spend their
marketing dollars and are concerned with maximizing its effects.

Clients are better equipped in measuring a campaign's
performance because they are armed with more sophisticated
digital tools—from metrics that measure a websites views, to a
viral video's or banner's performance, to a campaign's PR buzz
factor, to smart apps that employ advanced targeting systems
that deploy highly customized messages to very specific groups
or individual users. It's not enough to deliver good design and
great creative work—that's a given. The work must also possess an
intrinsic 360 degree strategy from its conceptual inception, created
with measurement and accountability in mind, on top of impact.

The best creatives I know play multiple roles, are strategic in their
thinking, account savvy in considering the work's metrics, as well
as production savvy with regard to seeking new ways of creating
that allow for new ways of seeing in order to warrant anyone's
attention. Once you earn the clients' trust and respect, they listen
more and view you as their brand partner. They know you have
their best interest in mind.

Q. Do you ever discuss budget with the creative team?
A. Budget is and will always be an issue, but it should never
hamper creativity. Creative solutions should always arise from the
brief, not a reaction to the budget. I'm a firm believer in "necessity
being the mother of all invention." Although budgets dictate what
you can and cannot do, the lack thereof can actually push you to
think harder, smarter, and perhaps even inspire you to think in a
different way, forcing you to reinvent the wheel.

Q. What should creative people remember about money?
1. Money and budgets are not the brief, but a means to an end.
2. Good creative will always sell itself. If you build it, they
   will come.

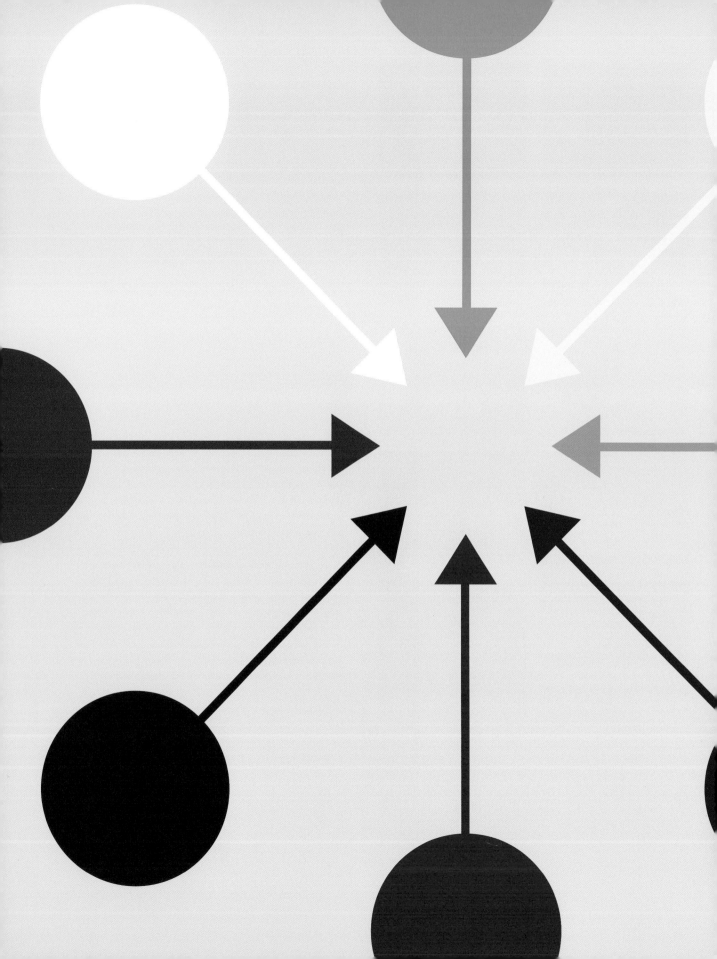

Chapter 5
Assembling the Team

Teamwork Basics

With the paperwork in order, the job budgeted and scheduled, and the creative brief in place, it's time to design. The question is, if it hasn't already been answered in the planning process, who exactly will be working on this project? Sometimes, this question is moot: For a solo designer or a small firm, the choices are limited. However, larger design firms may have multiple teams who can collaborate and who possess complementary skills—such as writers, web programmers, and photographers—to fulfill a project's requirements. It's a good way to boost expertise, but it also opens the door to complications, from financial to temperamental, which may need to be addressed. These are not insurmountable problems; they're just more details to be managed properly.

All design teams, large or small, require these things for optimum performance:

- Clear goals and objectives
- Unambiguous scope of work
- Well-defined expectations
- Delineated roles and responsibilities
- Relevant information and background for the project
- Sufficient time in which to work
- Appropriate technological tools
- Effective collaboration
- Ongoing communication
- Meaningful recognition and reward system
- Oversight and management support
- Consistent processes, from creative to communication
- Agreed-upon chain of command and functional authority

Team Composition

Typically, a project has a core design team consisting of a creative-focused and a client-focused professional. In many instances, more designers are added—some to take a hands-on creative role and some to provide more of a production or finishing capability. In addition, team members with a particular skill set may be added—for example, an illustrator or a print production manager. When a design firm gets larger, not only does the team expand, but there is also the option of adding administrative management personnel to help run the firm. They work to directly support creative and client service because they provide financial and administrative duties that make projects and the firm run better and more smoothly.

For any design team to work well together, each person needs to recognize that his or her performance affects the entire group in its ability to solve problems, develop creative, and satisfy the client. The more they understand what their contribution is to the project, the more attainable great results can be. When things are fuzzy and undefined, it's easy to believe it's someone else's responsibility to handle a certain task. Poor team performance often is the result of poor communication and an ineffective collaborative environment.

Job Descriptions and Activities

Optimally, a design firm should have personnel in three areas of focus: creative, client service, and operations. Project managers are typically working on a combination of tasks that could fall under any of these categories. Their role may best be diagrammed as the white triangle at the intersection of all three focus areas.

Creative
Creating the Work

Designer
Creative Director
Design Director
Photographer
Illustrator
Art Director
Engineer/Programmer
Copywriter

Client Service
Getting/Keeping the Work

Account Executive
Account Coordinator
Business Development
Strategist

Operations
Running the Business

Office Manager
Bookkeeper
Accountant
IT (Computers)
Admin/Clerical
Lawyer

Project Manager

The Creative Mix

Selecting the right creative people for a team can be challenging. Just because someone has relevant experience and a great portfolio doesn't ensure a wonderful fit. There are a variety of subjective factors to consider when choosing creative talent:

• Chemistry: Do you like this person?

• Style: Does this person fit in with the group?

• Attitude: Is the person positive or negative, cynical or enthusiastic?

• Design sensibility: Is it the same or different from ours?

• Professionalism: Is the person as buttoned up (or as loose) as the rest of the crew?

• Sense of humor: Does the person have one? (A little humor goes a long way in a stressful situation.)

• Temperament: Is it even-keeled? Will we have harmony with this person?

• Speed: Is the person used to a fast-paced or a slower environment? What's the person's approach?

Team Work Flow

Besides these personality-related factors, design teams need the right mix of skills and abilities. Design projects move from big-picture concepting to the highly detailed finished piece. This is achieved through a kind of "relay race," handing the project from content experts to aesthetic experts to technical experts, as the job moves from kickoff to completion (see chart below). Often, the only person constantly participating in the project is the project manager, who is involved in monitoring every aspect.

Every design team needs to be aware of and constantly be working to improve their teamwork, some aspects of which include

• Reliability

• Cooperation

• Knowledge sharing

Teams have obligations to each other and to the project they are working on. Project managers should bridge gaps and facilitate communication and work flow among team members. Project managers are the conduit that helps ease the difficulties of disparate personalities, expertise, and working styles.

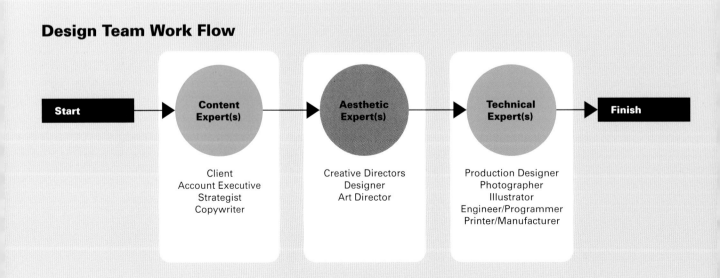

Design Team Work Flow

Start → **Content Expert(s)** → **Aesthetic Expert(s)** → **Technical Expert(s)** → **Finish**

Content Expert(s):
Client
Account Executive
Strategist
Copywriter

Aesthetic Expert(s):
Creative Directors
Designer
Art Director

Technical Expert(s):
Production Designer
Photographer
Illustrator
Engineer/Programmer
Printer/Manufacturer

Project Profile in Assembling the Team:

Objects of Affection designed by Sonnenzimmer / Chicago, Illinois USA

Objects of Affection Poster

Objects of Affection was a show featuring painters Anthony Adcock, Barbara Krol, and Jeff Stevenson, all members of the Chicago Artists Coalition. Each artist's work included realistically painted elements generally focused on one object—hence the title of the show. It was not easy to come up with a striking image that highlighted the show's concept, while not casting too big a shadow over the artists' work. Nick Butcher and Nadine Nakanishi, of Sonnenzimmer, rose to that challenge. "How do you advertise an art show you are not in? Our answer: nature!" says Butcher. "We started this poster with a photocopy of a crinkly greenish-brown leaf, using its shape to prime the paper for the following colors. From there, we used textures and painted elements to fill in the small sections of the leaf, creating a patchwork of color and shape."

RIGHT
The hand-screened poster is created on 19 × 25 inch (48.3 × 63.5 cm) acid-free archival paper and screen printed with nine different archival ink colors. The edition is only fifty prints and each one bears the embossed Sonnenzimmer mark. The piece features a subtle interplay of pleasing and balanced colors. The textures of the ink reveal details of the veins in the leaf and in the designs. "We love Nick and Nadine's work and trusted them with complete artistic license," explains artist Barbara Krol. "We simply provided them with the basic information and they took it from there."

Teamwork Responsibilities

Ask a seasoned designer the secret to team management, and he or she will say it is to get the right people doing the right job for the right client's project. Part of being able to select those people is to have a good creative brief, a well-defined scope of work, and an accurate deliverables list. From that comes a clear picture of what needs to be done. Match the right skill set, temperament, and perhaps most importantly, available talent, and you've got the perfect combination. Then it becomes a question of bringing these people into the project and getting to work.

In most design firms, the person obtaining, estimating, and planning the project is not the person who will design and implement it. Hopefully, the lead client service and creative team members have established the parameters and process required to complete the project. Out of this comes an understanding of who should be attached to the project.

Client Selects Team

Some design firms let the client choose the team. For example, the creative director allows the designers to develop concepts for a particular project. Then they do an internal critique and select the strongest ideas, which are presented to the client. The design direction the client approves is worked on by the people who created it. In that way, the client is choosing the team they want to work with. This methodology gives the whole staff a shot at each account. Other firms simply have the creative director make the staffing assignment based on anything from availability to serendipity.

Using Supplemental Staff

Each person on the design team should have a specific role and set of responsibilities. When the team is formed, this information and the assignment should be reviewed and confirmed. If the team member is on staff at the design firm, he or she should have a formal job description. Because of this, each person has a preexisting, broadly defined role or potential role in each project that comes into the firm. However, at the onset of each project, specific duties for each assignment need to be discussed with the worker.

Part of the team-assembly process is planning and then communicating the plan in a manner that everyone can understand. This is further complicated with the addition of team members from outside the firm, particularly if they seem to duplicate the core team's skills. An example is hiring a designer when there are already several on staff. However, not all designers are created equal: Some provide short bursts of creative energy, while others

Here are some things to consider when making personnel choices:

- Who has worked with this client before?
- Who has the relevant experience with a similar kind of project or client?
- Who would bring a fresh eye to the work?
- What technology is involved? Who has mastery of the technology required?
- What are the deliverables and the delivery media?
- Who needs a challenge, or a break, that this project would provide?
- How creative does this project need to be? Really experimental or very conservative?
- Who has the best stylistic and temperamental fit for this?
- Do we need a full- or part-time person?
- Who is available for the schedule that has been established?
- How much time does this project require of each person?

provide a reliable backup needed to see the project through to completion. For this reason, and maybe others, the team is sometimes supplemented with outside personnel.

Firm versus Project Hierarchy

Every design practice is different. Some have little or no hierarchy, with everyone reporting to the firm's owner; others have multiple layers of seniority and clear-cut divisions between departments. The structure that is right for the firm in terms of hierarchical rank may not hold true functionally in the day-to-day delivery of a particular design project. A creative director, for example, may be functionally accountable to a project manager well below his or her pay grade. The creative director empowers the project manager to advise him or her and to enforce agreed-upon work flow and project parameters, such as schedule or budget. In other instances, the firm's strict hierarchical structure applies within the realities of projects as well. This can make a project manager's job more difficult if a senior staff person refuses to report to him or her.

How the team functions is a matter of taste and efficiency. It is imperative, however, to communicate that structure so that all team members are clear on not only their roles and responsibilities, but others' as well. It is especially important for each team member to know who will review and approve their work. A firm can have a freewheeling creative collaborative culture, with designers supporting, brainstorming, and critiquing each other's work, but everyone needs to be clear on who makes the ultimate decisions that impact the design.

Case Study in Assembling the Team:

Wallace Church / New York, New York USA

Wallace Church, Inc., is a full-service strategic brand identity and package design firm. Over the past thirty-plus years, Wallace Church has helped to launch and renovate many leading brands from a range of product categories. Its commitment to marrying sound strategy with design solutions that stand out from the competition and engage consumers on many levels has contributed to the success of many brands. Stanley Church is the firm's founder, managing partner, and executive creative director. Rob Wallace is the managing partner and strategic director and is responsible for all brand imagery action plans and consumer research.

Lean Cuisine

One of Wallace Church's most prominent success stories is its work for Nestlé's Lean Cuisine line of frozen foods. "Our mission was threefold," explains Wallace. "Renovate to regain relevance for this stagnant 100+ SKU, $900 million (£623 million), twenty-plus-year-old brand; differentiate the product line to meaningfully separate it from diet food; and create impact by optimizing findability and shopability across multiple price segments." The charter was to make the brand more relevant to contemporary wellness cues, to determine the optimal hierarchy of product forms and flavors, and to launch a new product form, Spa Cuisine.

"Analysis showed that the old Lean Cuisine brand identity was trying too hard. To communicate a series of benefits, the brand perception was cluttered, complicated, and somewhat messy," notes Wallace. The old packaging did not communicate the strong emotional cues relevant for this leader in the wellness category. The prior design system used a number of fonts, a profusion of messages, and overstylized product photography.

BELOW

A new, cleaner photo aesthetic, a singular, simpler type strategy, a revitalized logo, and a more open architecture proved to best evoke desired perceptions and allow consumers to more easily identify the product at the store.

Simplifying the design architecture revitalized the Lean Cuisine brand, enhancing the brand's impact at retail and improving shopability. Increased sales prove that this new, simple design connects immediately and emotionally with consumers.

Sketches show the design development of the new branding and package design. Initial sales results indicate that Wallace Church's revitalized branding strategy was a successful driving force behind one of Nestlé's most successful product restages. Amanda Bach, Nestlé Prepared Foods Company's packaging communication design manager, states, "Simplifying the Lean Cuisine identity allowed us to recapture the brand's equities and drive shelf impact, and by color coding, helped enhance shopability. I believe this new, simpler, cleaner brand aesthetic will help consumers reconnect with the brand on an emotional level."

Case Study in Assembling the Team:

Wallace Church / New York, New York USA

Green Dahlia

The packaging for Green Dahlia chocolates is lush and artistically appealing. A rich, deep brown acts as a unifying color element to differentiate products and pull the eye toward the packaging. The visual language conveys a sense of being a premium product.

Dell

The Studio Hybrid is Dell's most sustainable, consumer-friendly and ecologically sensitive desktop computer. Wallace Church's challenge was to design a packaging concept that looks good, conveys a sense of being a "green" product that functions well on retail shelves, and can be shipped directly to customers in a small, efficient package—a lot to ask of one carton. Wallace Church executed beautifully on the brief, and the team was able to make Studio Hybrid's packaging from 95 percent recyclable materials so that it is curbside recyclable and closes the loop on the sustainability life cycle.

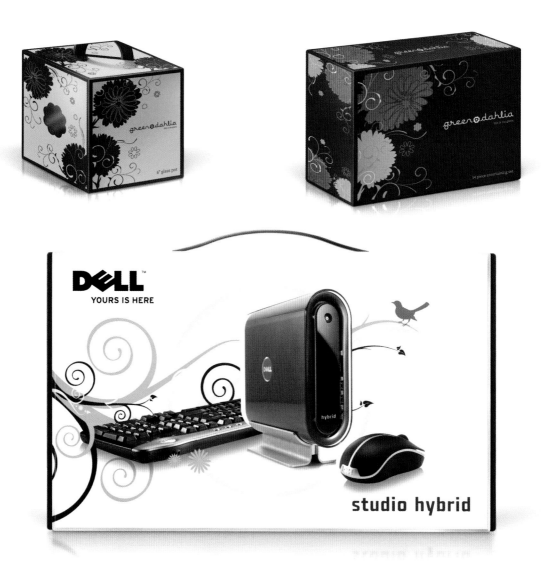

Dunkin' Donuts

Dunkin' Donuts is an international coffee and baked goods retailer that was founded in 1948 in Quincy, Massachusetts. It serves about 2.7 million customers per day at approximately 8,800 stores in thirty-one countries, including approximately 6,400 Dunkin' Donuts locations throughout the United States. Dunkin' Donuts is well known for its advertising, especially in its home region. Wallace Church worked with the brand to create special winter holiday promotional packaging.

Wallace Church used the well-established brand language and visual iconography to create the special winter holiday packaging. Donut boxes and coffee cups—the primary way customers experience the brand— were designed with bright circular graphics following Dunkin' Donuts' identity system.

"When in doubt: 'Think big, go small. Be smart, be simple.'"
—Rob Wallace, managing partner and strategic director, Wallace Church

Case Study in Assembling the Team:

Wallace Church / New York, New York USA

Suntory Iyemon Cha

When leading Japanese producer and distributor of spirits and beverages, Suntory Limited, wanted to introduce its new brand, Iyemon Cha, into the ice tea market, it called on Wallace Church to design the distinctive packaging. The brand needed to convey that this is a pure, all-natural beverage steeped in rich tea-making tradition. In fact, the world's finest green tea or "cha" comes from Kyoto, the ancient capital of Japan and the original source of Japanese green tea, which is where Iyemon Cha is made. Wallace Church's design hints at ancient roots but presents the brand in a refreshing, modern way.

Using a RACI Matrix for Design Team Management

One way to visualize and clarify the interdependent responsibilities of the design team is to create a RACI matrix, also sometimes called a responsibility assignment matrix (RAM). The following chart shows the various tasks required, the people involved, and the specific role they play in completion of various tasks. These roles are coded as follows:

R. (Responsible): Who does the work?
A. (Accountable): Who approves the work?
C. (Consulted): Who provides opinions/input about the work?
I. (Informed): Who gets a progress report on the work?

To make a RACI matrix useful, assign only one individual an "A" per task (i.e., hold only one person accountable). Multiple team members can be assigned "R," "C," or "I," however. These charts work well in a project's early stages as a planning and communication tool for teams.

This RACI matrix indicates roles and responsibilities for some of the tasks in phase 1 of a logo design project.

Sample RACI matrix

Phase 1: Logo Design

Task	Client	Account Executive	Creative Director	Designer Project	Manager
Kickoff Meeting	R	A	R	R	R
Client Interviews	I	A	R	R	C
Visual Audit	I	C	A	R	I
Competitive Landscape	I	A	C	R	I
Design Research	I	C	A	R	I

R Responsible **A** Accountable **C** Consulted **I** Informed

Six Characteristics of Successful Design Teams

1

Complementary skills

Team members are well matched but not identical copies of each other. There is a diversity of style, skills, experience, and ideas. A design team composed in this way is energetic, vital, and able to produce intriguing results. A project is enhanced by having a spectrum of design thinkers working together.

2

Empowered individuals

Everyone on the team, no matter how senior or junior, is encouraged to share opinions and ideas and is entrusted to do their job to the best of their ability. Empowered by the client and each other, designers can really flex their creative muscle.

3

Actively involved

Every team member is connected to the process and takes ownership of the design. Everyone feels they are making a real contribution and is passionately results focused.

Real unity

Team members respect and trust each other. Facilitated by ongoing communication and lots of listening, the team is open and committed to working as a group. This stems from collaborating often and achieving excellent outcomes.

Risk taking

Everyone, both individually and as a group, is willing to take chances, experiment, and push the envelope of what is possible in design. Trying new alternatives leads to innovation.

Civilized disagreement

Differences of opinion can lead to new ideas and add spice to the mix. Challenging the status quo and each other's beliefs can add to the process and enhance results. However, effective teams know when to resolve differences, agree to disagree, suppress unproductive conflict, and move on.

Virtual Teamwork

Not all design teams comprise members of the same firm collocated in the same office. Lots of design teams consist of people across several geographic locations, time zones, and even companies. Technology makes it possible to bring together interesting combinations of talented people. It's an exciting possibility, but like every other aspect of the design process, virtual teams require management.

In some ways, managing a virtual team is like managing people face to face, but a few things must be adjusted to make it work smoothly:

- Launching a project with a face-to-face meeting, if possible, is great for setting the proper tone and helping to facilitate a sense of personal connection among team members.
- Written forms of communication, such as email, can easily be shared and subsequently referred to later if necessary.
- Use of technology, especially web-based project management software, is a given.
- Being able to create virtual "war rooms" (i.e., collections of discovery materials held in one location) where people can review visual material and documents is essential.
- At some point, real-time viewing and discussion of work in progress must be facilitated.
- Some activities, such as brainstorming, may be better accomplished with shared physical proximity. Distance may slow certain processes, if not completely impede them.
- Camaraderie in design must be facilitated. Many elusive creative moments come from being in proximity to other creative people. Alternative scenarios need to be provided for this type of interaction to occur in some way.

Technology Tools for Teamwork

Virtual
Synchronous
• Telephone
• Text Messaging
• Webcams
• Videoconferencing

Collocated
Synchronous
• Face-to-Face Meeting
• File Sharing
• Telephone
• Instant Messaging

Asynchronous
• Email
• Voicemail
• Intranets
• Web-based Project Management Software

Asynchronous
• "War Rooms" (all materials posted in one place)
• Physical Job Jackets
• Library or Research Center
• Server Work Flow

Synchronous means working at the same time, while *asynchronous* means working at different times. Virtual teams are dispersed, while collocated teams are together in one place. This chart offers some ideas for tools that can help facilitate teams, no matter what their configuration.

- Verification of information must be pursued. Not everyone understands text-based messages. Voice inflection, as well as nonverbal communication, can often change the meaning of words. Managers need to make sure the team gets the right message.
- Teams that represent a variety of cultures—based on everything from ethnicity to geography to expertise in allied but different industries—can present a challenge, especially when none of their work time is face to face. Barriers come down when people can interact personally.
- Shared processes and agreed-upon work methods will bond the group. Having a team code of conduct will diminish misunderstandings and make the team more cohesive.

An asynchronous environment, in which team members and the client are not viewing and discussing the work simultaneously, can lead to lots of misunderstandings. Managing reactions and feedback becomes challenging in that context. Certain meetings, review sessions, and conferences should occur with all team members logging in or calling simultaneously. This is particularly important for initial creative concept presentations. Having the design team and the client participate directly with each other will allow real-time discussion, timely input, and group resolutions.

Tips for Working with Suppliers
Here are a few things to consider the next time you set out to find a collaborator or supplier:

- **Create depth of relationship together.**
  Sometimes, it makes more sense to put your eggs in fewer baskets. Go deep with certain suppliers and give them a lot of business and you get a loyal collaborator who speaks your language and understands how you like to work. Plus, they may give you discounts.

- **Look for suppliers when you don't need them.**
  Get referrals from clients and other designers. Get to know their abilities. Meet them face to face, if possible, to see if there is a rapport.

- **Bid efficiently.**
  Get organized. Anticipate the information they will need to create their estimates. Don't bluff if they ask a question you can't answer. Tell them you don't know, but you'll find out for them.

- **Bring them in as early as possible.**
  Let suppliers help you plan the work so that they can troubleshoot their part of the project. Leveraging their expertise early will make the project go smoother.

- **Treat them courteously.**
  Treat others the way you would want to be treated. Don't ask them for an estimate when you do not intend to hire them. Return their phone calls. Say thank you.

- **Understand that they have complementary skills.**
  They don't necessarily think like you do. Respect their knowledge and passion for their profession, which although allied to design, may be an entirely different field with its own concerns, processes, and standards. Get clarification if you don't understand them.

- **Don't burn bridges.**
  Suppliers talk to each other and word gets out which designers are impossible to work with or don't pay their bills. If you encounter an issue with a supplier, be honest. Work through the problems, such as payment plans for unpaid invoices, together.

Useful Questions for Screening Creatives

Whether you are hiring a staff designer or selecting a temporary collaborator for a project, you need to interview this person. Many design firms make hiring decisions based solely on portfolios. A lot of relevant information is contained in a portfolio: Style sensibility, attention to detail, quality, and experience are all obvious. But what else can you uncover about the person behind the work that would help you make an informed choice? Here are some openended questions to ask:

- What was your last project? What did you learn from it? What did you like and dislike about it?
- Describe your work process on a typical project. How do you approach design?
- Which pieces in your portfolio are you most proud of? Why?
- What kinds of clients do you prefer to work with? Why? Which clients in your portfolio were like this? Which ones were not?
- What kind of creative direction did you have on this particular project? How do you like to be supervised? What make a good boss?
- What are your professional goals? Where do you see yourself in five years?
- What do you think are your strong and weak points? What are your plans to improve your deficiencies and enhance your strengths?
- What organizations or activities do you pursue that enrich you as a designer? What professional societies are you a member of and how have they helped your career?

Remember that these questions are meant to aid in discussions that reveal more about the person you are interviewing. However, it is against the law in many countries to discriminate on the basis of gender, age, ethnicity, region, sexual orientation, skin color, or national origin, so steer clear of any conversations that touch on those topics.

Project Profile in Assembling the Team:

Magabala Diary designed by Finn Creative / Kunnamura, Australia

Magabala Diary

Celebrating more than twenty years of publishing about indigenous Australians, Magabala Books, in conjunction with Finn Creative, created a distinctive cross-cultural daily diary showcasing aboriginal and Torres Strait Islander storytellers, writers, and illustrators through exquisite portraits, book excerpts, and artist profiles. Finn Creative is lead by creative director Kevin Finn. Prior to moving to Australia, Irish-born Finn worked in Dublin and New Zealand with top design studios. He then spent seven years as joint creative director at Saatchi Design, Sydney, winning national and international recognition.

Project Profile in Assembling the Team:

Magabala Diary designed by Finn Creative / Kunnamura, Australia

The Magabala desk diary is both a revenue stream for the company, and a promotional item. "Early in the process, I suggested that we may be able to include a number of other levels to the diary," says Finn. "For a start, we should look at how indigenous people view the calendar year, and also include dates that have particular significance for indigenous people. Added to this, since Magabala produces books, I felt it would be interesting for users to have access to excerpts to the authors' works as this would make the diary more engaging (and more valuable) as well as promoting the authors (and, in turn, Magabala Books)."

"One of my goals was to try to make the diary as cross-cultural as possible, as well as perhaps making it a resource to further educate about indigenous culture," Finn explains. "In addition to this, a key objective is to access people who may not normally see themselves as having an interest in aboriginal culture, simply because the usual portrayal of aboriginality is delivered through painting—dot painting in particular. Creating a diary that on the one hand is smart and sophisticated looking and on the other hand provides a wider look at aboriginal culture through literature, became a critical objective. Above all, the desk diary needed to be practical."

Since Magabala Books produces books, the visual direction was based in this truth. All the Magabala Books–related information, including the authors' backgrounds and excerpts, are delivered as though inside a small book contained in the diary. The diary will be produced each year, so it needs to remain consistent but fresh each year. The book idea will be the constant (almost template) for each diary.

"The Western calendar is linear and very fixed, split into days and months," notes Finn. "The indigenous calendar is circular, fluid, and flexible, split into seasons that are defined by when flora and fauna appear or disappear and are dictated by weather patterns. Even though the Western calendar is specific (365.25 days to be exact), we still commonly use the phrase 'the whole year round.' And even though the Western calendar is linear, once December 31 comes around, the next day starts the process from the beginning again, so it also has a cyclical nature."

Chapter 6
Managing Creatives

Creatively Managing Creative People

Managing people is an art form, and design project managers need this skill. They need to be able to determine and implement budgets and schedules, as well as handle the people on the team.

Managers working with creative directors and design firm owners need to utilize the workforce in a way that results in great creative and maximum productivity—two things that can seemingly be at cross purposes during certain projects. Productivity, broadly speaking, is output per hour of labor or work. The highest cost on any design project, or for the design firm, will always be the design team's salaries. So, in graphic design, it's all about utilizing the team's abilities in a way that consistently allows for the best, most useful, and creative output possible.

Evaluating Employees

Many things influence the productivity of a design team, including project work conditions (job complexity and type), nonproductive activities (impediments such as miscommunication, bad client input, computer problems, health issues, etc.), and labor characteristics (worker quality and contribution). *The PMBOK Guide* (see page 14) cites the following factors as useful when evaluating workers and their performance:

- Quality of work
- Quantity of work
- Job knowledge
- Related work knowledge
- Judgment
- Initiative
- Resource utilization
- Dependability
- Analytical ability
- Communication ability
- Interpersonal skills
- Ability to work under pressure
- Safety consciousness (for a design team: creative consciousness)
- Profit and cost sensitivity
- Planning effectiveness
- Leadership
- Delegating
- Development of other people

The PMBOK Guide suggests assessing each item on a three-point scale. The lower the score is, the better the employee is.

3 = Needs improvement
2 = Meets expectations
1 = Recognized strength

As we all know, brilliant creativity on demand isn't always possible. Some things take a little longer to get right. However, professional graphic designers work hard to close this gap and produce great work consistently and efficiently. So much of ensuring that this will occur has to do with making sure you have the right people for the right job. Ask yourself:

• Do they clearly understand the creative brief and the project's goals?
• Do they have the technical skills we need?
• Do they have the creative abilities required for this project?
• Are their time management skills up to par?
• Do they have a good attitude about this project and the team members assigned to it?

Bring Out the Best

A clearly defined leader who directs the work with a well-conceived and articulated vision can bring out the best in a design team. This person tends to inspire the team to be more creative, take informed risks, and push to be the best they can be. Some other factors that bring out the best in creative people include

• Mutual respect
• Acknowledgment of people's contributions, including credit
• Good working conditions
• Challenging and exciting work
• Opportunities for growth
• Rewards, financial and otherwise

Sometimes, design firms don't want their employees to be overly creative but, rather, to be creative within a certain bandwidth of what a client expects the firm to produce. This is an important conversation to have with employees. Being creative within the project's agreed-upon parameters (as stated in the creative brief) and within the inevitable project constraints is critical and is a major aspect of what separates designers who are in it for the business and designers who are in it for the art form. It could be that exercising full creativity is optimal when working on the firm's self-promotion pieces.

Put It in Writing

One of the best things a design firm can do to ensure that the staff is working up to expectations is to have a contract or a letter of agreement setting forth expectations about the working relationship and outlining employees' job responsibilities and what they can expect in return for this work. Include the following in any employment agreement you have with your staff:

• Hire date
• Terms of employment (hours/days of work, sick leave, holidays, vacation time, etc.)
• Full job description
• Salary
• Benefits (health insurance, professional memberships, training/educational opportunities, retirement savings plan, etc.)
• Performance review process outline
• Date of first performance review
• Dated signature of employer
• Dated signature of employee

Design firm owners frequently complain that staff members aren't doing what they should be, or they emphasize the wrong activities. This is usually due to a communication problem. Prioritize each employee's duties and responsibilities in his or her employment agreement. Then have the design project manager further monitor the team members' work to ensure that they are doing the right job in the context of a particular project.

Choosing a Leadership Style

How you lead is a function of your temperament, character, beliefs, style, and situational circumstances. What works at one time may not work at another. Understanding some basics about leadership styles will provide you with choices.

Some forces that influence the leadership style to be used include
• How much time is available for the project or task at hand?
• Is the relationship with the group based on respect and trust?
• Who has the relevant information?
• How well trained or expert are the group members?
• Are there any internal conflicts?
• What are the group's stress levels?
• Is the task structured or unstructured, complex or simple?

In the 1930s, social psychologists at the University of Iowa, led by Kurt Lewin, identified three styles of leadership based on decision making. Their experiments with groups of children working on arts and crafts projects showed that human behavior is a product of a person's internal make-up, but it is greatly affected by the dynamic environment the person is in. These styles and expected outcomes are described on the opposite page.

Leadership Style

Type 1: Autocratic (Directive, Authoritarian)

- Centralizes authority
- Dictates work methods
- Makes unilateral decisions without consulting others
- Limits employee participation and input
- Clear division between leader and followers

Works well when

- There is no need for input in the decision.
- The decision won't or can't change as a result of input.
- The motivation to do subsequent activities won't be affected by whether the group was involved in the decision.
- There is no time for group decision making.
- The leader is the most knowledgeable member of the group.
- The employee doesn't know his or her job.

Impact (Pro and Con):

- Provides clear expectation of what to do and when and how to do it
- Is highly effective when used rarely
- Causes the highest level of discontent
- Leads to revolution if autocratic leadership is excessive
- Is viewed as controlling, bossy, and dictatorial if the style is abused

Type 2: Democratic (Participative)

- Delegates authority, empowers others
- Involves employees in decision making
- Encourages participation in deciding work methods
- Uses feedback as an opportunity to coach employees
- Typically leads to greater acceptance of decisions

Two versions of the style:

- Consultative: seeks input, but makes the final decision
- Participative: operates in group mode, leader is just another member

Works well when

- You want employees to be engaged in and more committed to the process.
- Employees are motivated and creative.
- There is time to gain group input.
- You have part of the information and your employees have the other part.

Impact (Pro and Con):

- Most effective style with the majority of groups
- Usually appreciated by the group, especially if they have had autocratic leadership in the past
- Seen as a sign of the leader's strength and respect for others
- Problematic when there is a wide range of opinions and no clear way to reach an equitable solution

Type 3: Laissez-Faire (Delegative, Free Reign)

- Abdicates authority
- Gives employees complete freedom to make decisions
- Allows employees to work as they see fit
- Provides materials and answers questions, but delegates alternatively, offers no guidance
- Minimizes the leader's involvement, although the leader is still responsible for the outcome

Works well when

- Employees are capable and motivated.
- The group is composed of experts in diverse fields.
- You have full confidence in your employees to get the work done right.
- No coordination is required.

Impact (Pro and Con):

- Allows highly qualified expert employees to determine what to do and how to best do it
- Results in employees who often don't put in as much energy as when they are actively led
- Results in groups that are less productive than if led with other styles
- Results in poorly defined roles

Case Study in Managing Creatives:

Umbrella Design / Mumbai, India

Umbrella is a specialty design house, one of the very few in India. Umbrella's portfolio consists of corporate identity, retail design, advertising, and corporate communications. The firm is led by Managing Director Bhupal Rhamnathkar, Executive Creative Director Deven Sansare, and COO Farhad F. Elavia. Umbrella has worked with top international and regional clients, and often acts as a launching pad for young talent. "We're a relatively new company," explains Sansare. "Given that we are small and independent, we tend to prefer younger designers who are affordable. Our approach is 'Take what you get and train and guide them.' Mentoring then becomes a necessity. Using freelancers has been a part of the setting-up strategy."

Pallavi Jaikisshan

Pallavi Jaikisshan is a noted Indian fashion designer, known for bridal dresses, often with an intriguing take on conventional styles and structures. Jaikisshan's collection is aimed at giving a modern flavor to bridal traditions. Asked how that is achieved, she replies, "Most of my dresses look like classy evening gowns. I give them a twist without ignoring Indian sensibilities." Umbrella worked with Jaikisshan to create an identity and ads for the brand.

ABOVE
"We were hired to do the logo," explains Sansare. "The script typography takes its inspiration from wedding invitations often seen in India."

RIGHT
Once the new identity was created, the client asked Umbrella to design ads for her latest collection, which included nonbridal collection apparel. The choice of non-Indian models in the ads reflects the premium and desirability of Western-looking faces to sell products to Indian consumers.

Marriott U magazine

"It began with a phone call," recalls Sansare. "The marketing director of Marriott Group in India wanted to combine monthly and bimonthly newsletters that various properties send out into one quarterly magazine. We made our first presentation a week later, not just as designers but as a team that understood brand Marriott. We suggested the nature of editorial content, the kind of advertisers to target, and names for the magazine. Every recommendation was based on the Marriott proposition 'Spirit to Serve' and its image as a luxury brand in India."

The creative team suggested the name *U* because it captured the customer-centric proposition of the brand. The editorial content suggestion, summed up in this one sentence, "We should not talk about holidays to exotic islands but about how to buy an exotic island," was also accepted by Marriott. Then, while the client scouted for an editorial team, Umbrella got down to designing the masthead and cover design.

"We concepted with the photographer, stylist, and costume designer, to shoot a Bollywood actress for the cover and other models who would be shot in the various properties," explains Sansare, "all while our designers were trying to crack a design for the editorial sections that would be dictated by fixed column widths (like any other magazine), and yet be dynamic enough to change with every issue."

A team of three designers worked on the *Marriott U* magazine—one senior, two junior—and all reported to Ramnathkar. Two writers were involved: a junior and a writer-creative director (Sansare). The project was coordinated by a senior account executive. Umbrella also created the print-ready artwork and their print and production head coordinated with the paper suppliers and printers.

Case Study in Managing Creatives:

Umbrella Design / Mumbai, India

Bates

Bates is an advertising agency born in Asia. In fact, its full name used to be Bates Asia. With time, it was taken over by international advertising giant, WPP Group. Bates had been creating subdivisions to keep in step with the rapidly changing mediascape and the emergence of digital media so that it could offer clients an integrated communication solution. 141, from one-for-one, was one division that was involved in new media activation, a business that Bates saw as the

future. Soon after, Bates decided to drop the "Asia" suffix and replace it with "141" in what it saw as a combination of its brand equity (Bates) and its future focus (141).

Asia-devoted marketing communications network operating in fifteen countries with twenty-two offices. The Bates 141 philosophy is centered on "change," with the agency calling itself "The Change Agency." This philosophy is based on the agency's ability to change consumers, channels, tastes, and

values by changing mindsets and behaviors. The company calls the region in which it operates "The Asias." This is to recognize that the region is home to more than half of the world's population, and as such, sweeping generalizations should not be made about the people who live there.

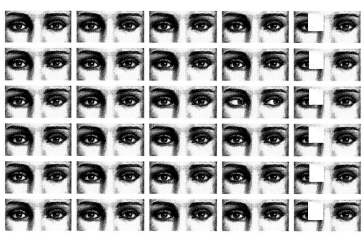

Managing Creative People at Umbrella Design

"We work on two insights, really," says Umbrella Design executive creative director Deven Sansare. "Here are some things we consider:

1. Good creative people are highly competitive. When they see their boss do great work, it usually brings out the best in them
2. Everybody needs a father and mother. If they believe that their failures will be shouted at but accepted and their successes will be rewarded, then most of the time you don't really need to 'manage' them."

Case Study in Managing Creatives:

Umbrella Design / Mumbai, India

Another challenge Umbrella took on for Bates 141 was to extend the identity to individual office environments. "We took the easy way out: We chose the Mumbai office for the pilot," admits Sansare. "Its interiors were designed in coordination with an interior designer and under our supervision. This office design then created a template for the other offices to follow. So far, the Hong Kong, Singapore, Philippines, and Vietnam offices have been redesigned."

Manosh Mukherjee
EP0040

Sandhya Garg
EP0054

Amrish Desai
EP0042

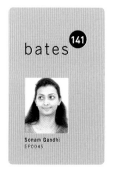

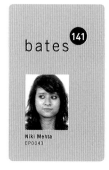

Priyanshu Chattergee
EP0055

Sonam Gandhi
EP0045

Nevil Loyola
EP0057

Niki Mehta
EP0043

Mine

"One of our clients is a company that cuts, polishes, and exports diamonds," says Rhamnathkar. "It has two other subsidiaries. One manufactures and exports diamond jewelry; the other manufactures it and supplies it to retailers in India. They tied up with a Kerala-based chain of jewelry stores and launched their own brand of diamond jewelry that would have its own section in these stores. The long-term ambition was to have exclusive stores for the brand. Our initial task was to come up with a name. We came up with one that was based on a fact and a feeling—Fact: You find diamonds in a mine. Feeling: Pride that this piece of diamond jewelry is mine. The brand name: Mine."

BELOW
Umbrella created a presentation that consisted of
1. The brand graphic created using the distinctive circle in the Mine logo
2. A color and texture palette
3. Material recommendations
4. Brand guidelines
5. Reference images
This presentation became the foundation of the brief to the interior designer that worked on Mine's retail environments. That gave the client tangible parameters to judge the store layouts, design, displays, and materials. From then on, it was a simple supervision job for the design agency and the client. The first exclusive Mine store is in Bangalore.

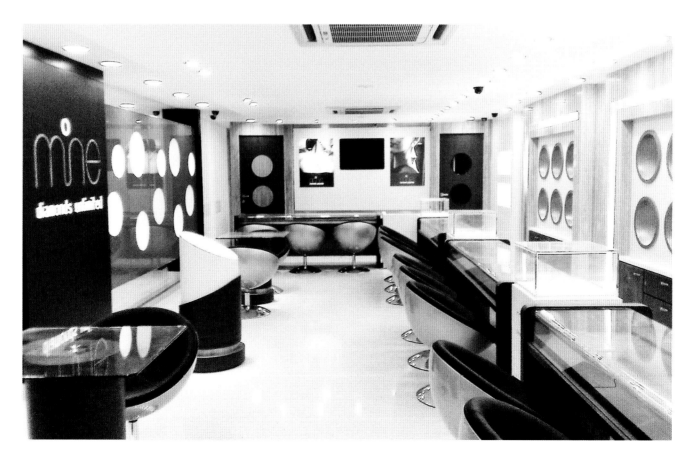

Working Well Together

Many design teams don't clearly understand each other's roles and responsibilities. Some don't have the benefit of good leadership and management. That needs to change to both gel as a team and be able to do great design. Everyone on the design team needs to hold each other accountable to achieve optimum performance.

One of the realities of graphic design is that as projects move from concept to completion, they are in the hands of many experts—or in the case of a solo freelance designer one person is performing a variety of activities. Traditionally, the design work flow starts with the highly creative expert and ends with the highly technical expert. Experience and skill levels vary, but so does specific design expertise. Those who come up with great ideas can't always execute them. Different skills are required as the process progresses from rough idea to finished piece. A designer should explain this to the client, but also make it clear within the design team. Projects are usually better served when handled by the team member with the most expertise in that phase of work. This disaggregating of design tasks allows the best person to be focusing talent on a particular aspect.

This chart shows the major roles of most design teams. Obviously, larger multipart projects could require additional people (more people in these roles, plus others such as illustrators, photographers, animators, and programmers). Design teams must understand that they will be working collaboratively with numerous people, often with different views of the project. Here again, respect is key.

Outlining a Team's Responsibilities

Roles	Responsibilities
Client	Initiates the job and provides project requirements and background information. Frames the creative brief. Approves project deliverables and verifies that they meet requirements.
Client Contact (Account Executive)	Handles new-business acquisition or sales. Provides account service, including daily phone contact with client. Advises project manager.
Estimator/ Proposal Writer	May be the client contact or the project manager. Handles all financial negotiations, paperwork setup.
Creative Director	Provides big-picture vision. Typically writes the creative brief and defines the strategy. Does client presentations. Assigns the creative team.
Project Manager	Manages the project. Creates various plans related to the project. Measures project performance, takes corrective action, controls project outcomes, manages project team, and reports project status.
Designer	Designs the piece per the creative brief. Responsible for completing project activities and producing deliverables.
Copywriter	Writes the piece per the creative brief. Responsible for completing text content.
Production Artist (Production Designer)	Creates finished files based on the designer's approved design.
Production Manager	Bids and manages the fabrication of the design.
Bookkeeper	Provides all job-related invoices, manages cash flow, and handles the money.
Suppliers	Provide goods or services to assist project team in completing the project.

How to Effectively Critique Design

At some point in all projects, the design will be critiqued, both internally and externally. Some design firms ask the design team to critique the design as well. Here are some steps and questions to guide a team's feedback and responses to a design during a critique:

Step 1: Overview
▶ Initial reactions: What is your first impression of the design?
▶ Content: Is the design complete?
▶ Aesthetics: What is the overall effect? Does it feel right?
▶ Style: Is the design appropriate for the stated goal or purpose?

Step 2: Analysis
▶ Layout: Does everything seem to be in the right place?
▶ Flow: Does the content appear in a natural and logical progression?
▶ Usability: Is it easy to use or interact with the design?
▶ Typography: Does the type feel appropriate in tone?
▶ Color: How is color being used? How does it convey the desired message?
▶ Missing: Is anything missing? Is anything there that shouldn't be?

Step 3: Interpretation
▶ Audience: How do you think the target audience will respond to this design? Why?
▶ Details: Is the use of graphic elements consistent with the design goals? Why? Why not?
▶ Problem areas: What things in this design are not as effective as they could be? Why do you think that?
▶ Appeal: Is this an effective and appealing design for its context? Why? Why not?

Step 4: Evaluation
▶ Creative brief: Does this design fulfill the goals of the creative brief? If not, why not?
▶ Judgment: Given the answers to these questions, does this design work?

Case Study in Managing Creatives:

Sterling Brands / New York, New York, and San Francisco, California USA

Sterling Brands is a leading brand and design identity firm, formed in 1992 with a staff of ninety professionals in the United States. The firm has been responsible for branding some of the most well-known products in the world. Sterling Brands also has affiliate offices in Singapore and London and is a member of the Omnicom Network.

Stop and Shop: Simply Enjoy

To launch a new premium line of private label products, Stop & Shop, a leading U.S. supermarket retailer, asked Sterling to create a new name and package design that would clearly distinguish the brand from other private label products, as well as from other premium products on its shelves. "We named the line Simply Enjoy to articulate the idea of great food made simple and created a sophisticated design that highlights each product's premium ingredients," explains Debbie Millman, president of Sterling's Design Group in New York.

For Simply Enjoy, Sterling Brands provided innovation including developing the brand name, architecture design, packaging, identity, signage system, and guidelines.

Case Study in Managing Creatives:

Sterling Brands / New York, New York, and San Francisco, California USA

Pepperidge Farm

Sterling worked with long-time client Pepperidge Farm in redesigning its signature Distinctive Cookies line to help increase its equity as the primary brand for premium, casual entertaining. To contemporize and elevate the attributes of the line, photography showcases the unique shape of the cookies, while accent garnishes reinforce flavor and distinguish each variant. The iconic white background is elegant and warm, reflecting the brand's heritage.

Ben & Jerry's

Unilever wanted to refresh the iconic Ben & Jerry's ice cream brand by redesigning the packaging graphics for the product line. The major goal was to clarify the various Ben & Jerry's line segments, flavors, and products, while retaining valued brand equities. Sterling's contemporary, revitalized package design brings back the heart and soul of the brand, creates a stronger presence for the brand in the freezer cabinet, and makes it easier to find the individual flavors.

> "Our internal culture is a critical aspect of our business. It is the most unique and enduring quality about Sterling Brands. Like all successful project-based businesses, we have a high metabolic rate that energizes and inspires our clients."
> —Debbie Millman, president, Sterling Brands Design Group

Mally

To launch celebrated makeup artist
Mally Roncal's line of cosmetics, Sterling
Brands created a design that blends attributes
reflecting a feminine style with an edgy
and sassy sensibility. This approach reflects
Roncal's personality and sense of style.
The visual toolbox developed for the
brand includes soft pink and green hues
combined with a snakeskin texture.

Lip Illusion
lip magnifier

Total Net Wt.: .18 oz./5.2 g

Perfecting Blush

Net Wt.: .09 oz./2.55 g

Case Study in Managing Creatives:

Sterling Brands / New York, New York, and San Francisco, California USA

Benjamin Moore

"On an on-going basis, Sterling helps Benjamin Moore redefine the paint category and connect with the people who live with their brand every day," explains Millman. "We have developed names and package design for such innovative subbrands as Ben, Aura Exterior, Natura, and the contractor program, Inside Edge. Each name and design considers the lifestyle choices consumers make as they turn to this brand—as a catalyst for their creativity and as an expression of their style." The products shown here reflect Sterling's recent work, which included innovation, naming, visual and subbrand strategy, identity, and package design.

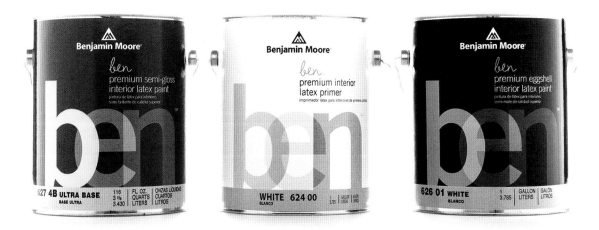

Team Management Issues

Even with the best of intentions, lots of designers don't always play well with others. This may stem from having an independent creative nature. Couple that with the thrill of the hunt as they chase ideas and pursue innovative design solutions, and hours or days can go by before a designer looks up from the computer and checks in with others. In reality, that doesn't work well, and designers probably should not be left alone without supervision. However, it must be useful supervision. This is why design managers need to figure out an unobtrusive yet effective way to monitor the team's work.

Here are some of the main causes for wasted time and inefficiency that a project manager must be vigilant about:
• Poor planning
• IT or computer problems
• Mismatch of skills to required tasks
• Inadequate team supervision
• Poor communication

Culture and Communication

It is most desirable to develop a culture within a design firm that nourishes creativity and business. Good project management can assist in that goal. One of the most powerful tools a manager can utilize is great communication. Here are some communication activities that a project manager should engage in on an ongoing basis:
• Reporting project status to all stakeholders—design team and clients
• Reporting on changes to the project, especially scope of work changes or content revisions
• Reporting major concerns—team complaints and various obstacles

Through these activities, the manager is taking an objective view of the project's work flow and keeping everyone well informed. It is then up to each team member to utilize what has been communicated to do their best work.

Giving Feedback

Do
▶ Give feedback when asked.
▶ Consider your response carefully before speaking.
▶ Be specific and concise.
▶ Tie objections to a clear rationale; put comments in context.
▶ Notice the body language of the person you're talking to.
▶ Encourage discussion and useful debate.
▶ Make sure the person understands your feedback.
▶ Think of solutions or alternatives if invited to participate.

Don't
▶ Get emotional; keep it professional.
▶ Attack the person; challenge his or her thinking instead.
▶ State opinions as though they were facts.
▶ Walk away if the person wants further discussion.
▶ Get defensive if the person doesn't like your feedback.
▶ Demand it be done your way simply to power-trip someone.
▶ Provide a new solution or alternative if it isn't your job to do so.

Solo-abriation:
Ten Reasons Why Your Last Collaboration Didn't Work
By Marshall Rake

Whether you are fresh out of design school or a professional with more than twenty years of experience, at some point, you have collaborated. And if you are anything like me, half of those collaborations failed miserably. The good ones produce the best work of your career, and the bad ones make you age horribly and keep you up at night questioning your profession. Successful collaborations force us to learn from one another. They make designers grow by testing their limits. Collaborations are what being a designer is all about. Here are ten reasons why collaboration can fail:

1. Ego
If you are the more talented designer in the group, keep your ego in check and get the other person involved. Give the person small tasks that keep him or her contributing. Collaborations can succeed only if all parties involved are feeding off each other. If neither of you has anything to offer the other, there is no reason to have a partner.

2. Brief Interpretations
Every designer brings a different frame of reference to the table. What is obvious to you may not be obvious to the person you are working with. Make sure you take the time to clearly go over the client's and the project's goals.

Type it out. It is always good to have something physical to refer to. When the arguments and differences begin to mount up, this will be the squabble solver.

3. Bad project
Sometimes, it really is not your fault. This may not be the most popular viewpoint in the world, but every project cannot be the best piece of design ever made. Sometimes, all you can do is make something bad a little better. If you do that, you do your job. You won't win the awards, but you'll make some logo for some small coffee shop in some small town just a tiny bit better.

4. Unfamiliar relationship
Collaboration is just like any other relationship in your life. You need to know what the other person is all about, and he or she needs to know what you are all about. Just because you have seen their portfolio does not mean you know them. Your project has a three-week deadline, but the pieces in their portfolio could have taken three months. Understand their work and not their glossy portfolio.

Talk about the project over lunch, coffee; anything that gets you out of the studio and talking. The more you know about them, the better.

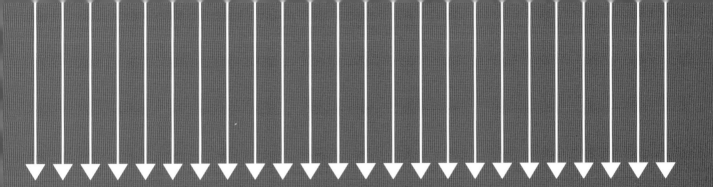

5. Work habits

You know how you work, you like how you work. You are a diligent designer, you work hard and you stay focused. Your partner relies on Hail Marys and all-nighters. The collaboration is a short-term marriage; make it work!

Be the bigger person. Adjust to your partner's schedule. Sacrifice yourself for the good of the project.

6. Work schedule

Your place or mine? Early or late? What exactly is early? It is hard enough balancing one person's schedule; now you have to balance two.

It is not necessary to always work in the same room. When starting the project, it is helpful to physically work together to establish the relationship. Once you both are on the same page, feel free to work on your own, but do not overlook the importance of checking in face to face.

7. Designer-to-client relations

We are in the people business. Communication with clients can make or break the project. Handle the client well and they begin to trust you and the project will become infinitely more enjoyable.

Pick one collaborator to communicate with the client. Work as one united front. Send all the emails from one account; place all phone calls from one number. Keep it simple; do not confuse the client.

8. Inhibition

Speak up. If you have a good idea, let your partner know. Do not be afraid to be rejected. If you do not speak up and you are unhappy with how the project is turning out, you only have yourself to blame. It is your project, too; you should like it.

9. Base Knowledge

We did not all attend the same school, look at the same books, or have the same software and professional training. Do not assume everyone understands things the way you do; in fact, assume no one else knows exactly what you know. You might have to explain things to your partner, and he or she might have to do the same to you.

Be patient, and if you do not know, just ask. Collaborations are a great chance to learn.

10. Communication

You can avoid all of the previous issues by doing one simple thing: communicating. Be open and up front. If everyone involved knows exactly what is going on and exactly what needs to be done, the collaboration will be enjoyable and fruitful.

The next time you start a brand-new collaboration, keep these things in mind and just maybe you will come out a little happier, and a little richer.

Marshall Rake is a graphic designer and writer based in New York City. You can see his design work at www.marshallrake.com; and his literary and current culture publication, *Epilogue*, which can be seen at www.epiloguemagazine.com.

Project Profile in Managing Creatives:

BBC2 designed by Guilherme Marcnondes / Los Angeles, California USA + São Paulo, Brazil

Brazilian-born Guilherme Marcondes has worked with a number of stellar design studios around the world, creating work that blurs the frontiers between genres, techniques, and media. "I think it's more inspiring when things fall between traditional definitions," Marcondes says. "When you do something and you can't explain if it's 'animation' or 'film,' if it's 'humor' or 'horror,' that's when it starts to get interesting for me." That's what he did for BBC2 television network spots to promote Bruce Parry, one of the network's most popular show hosts.

This spot was one in a series of six (each directed by a different person) promoting some of the hosts of BBC2's popular shows. "I love the miniature approach, with its rustic metal parts and plastic plants, lending this piece a tactility that cannot be matched with any high-end 3-D/VFX wizardry," says Marcondes.

Marcondes concepts the idea behind his films first, then chooses a combination of techniques to achieve his vision. "This spot was for Bruce Parry, who presents some wild reality shows, such as *Tribe* and *Amazon*," he says. "My job was to create a visual interpretation of Bruce's concerns about the environment and life in a materialistic society."

These images show behind-the-scenes and early production material from the Bruce Parry Identity for BBC2. "We built the 'ultimate exploitation machine,' powered by human beings, ravaging the land, sucking nature on one side and spitting out consumer goods on the other," says Marcondes. "We placed the scene inside a mirror box to create a sense of boundlessness to the destructive process imposed by the machine."

Marcondes' work is rich in texture and symbolism. It is both bizarre and beautiful in its hybrid of story-telling techniques.

The spot for Bruce Parry took about forty-five weeks to accomplish—three weeks for preproduction, one day to shoot, and two weeks for postproduction work.

"My client was into the idea, so I didn't have a lot of challenges on the creative front. Close to the delivery date, I had some problems with BBC2 executives, complaining that the spot turned out too 'strange.' I had to make some last-minute changes I disagreed with, but it turned out okay. I learned that you have to push the limit right at the beginning of the project. The tendency is that it becomes more watered down as you move into production."
—Guilherme Marcondes, designer/director

Perfectionism

Perfectionism is about striving to be the best. In its healthiest form, perfectionism can drive a designer toward new and exciting work. When it is unhealthy, however, it leads to obsession and anxiety.

Since so many graphic designers regularly experience a kind of perfectionism, design managers need to have a working understanding of the condition and a plan to circumvent it. There's sometimes a fine line between healthy and unhealthy drives toward perfectionism and graphic design. Here are some of the pros and cons.

Pros:

- Adaptive perfectionists are healthy, focused strivers, and very alert.
- People with obsessive personality types are into perfectionism. They are focused. This is not to be confused with Obsessive Compulsive Disorder (OCD), which is a clinical psychological disorder involving various ritualized behaviors.
- These people get a sense of pleasure from their work, especially their painstaking efforts.
- They are often workaholics who are high achievers.
- They are very motivated and persevere in the face of obstacles and discouragement, which can be inspiring to others. They are committed to overcoming roadblocks and pitfalls that stop others.
- They pay meticulous attention to detail, a commitment that pushes them toward excellence.
- They're driven to make reality match their concepts.
- They want to be the best. They are vigilant and dedicated, and possess high personal standards and lofty expectations about themselves and their team's abilities.
- They strive for excellence, and enjoy achieving that excellence and feeling good about accomplishments and lessons learned, all of which works to deepen their confidence.
- They're tough on themselves and others, but are not afraid to fail. They take informed risks and push themselves.
- They're incredibly productive—they are always in action and ready for new challenges.
- They are okay with trial and error on the road to success.

What it means to a design manager:
These people can be inspiring. They have an ideal, but accept that it is a guideline or goal to propel the team forward. They are not defeated if these goals are not achieved 100 percent. It means they are still achieving above and beyond what others who don't go for it achieve.

What to do:
Encourage their playfulness and willingness to tackle a big challenge— that's the breeding ground of innovation. This kind of perfectionism boosts creativity. However, monitor the situation carefully, and make sure the drive toward excellence doesn't become a perfectionism trap. Keep them focused on the creative brief. Always remind the team of their goals. Applaud meaningful results.

Cons:

- Maladaptive perfectionists are neurotic and often have OCD.
- They're unable to feel satisfied with their work because they can't see a job well done; they only see problems and flaws.
- They may avoid situations where they might be seen as imperfect or a failure—this means they play it safe and don't seek risk.
- They can procrastinate because of fear of mistakes or errors. This stems from their deep fear of rejection.
- They can become intensely anxious because of their fear. They feel it is unacceptable to make a mistake.
- They are obsessive and they must be in control at all times. They try to anticipate everything so that they can protect themselves and others against unforeseen circumstances. In doing so, they often wear themselves out.
- They put a lot of pressure on themselves and others.
- They are often workaholics who can't relax.
- They can be extremely sensitive to criticism, yet stubborn, confrontational, and hypercritical of others.
- They can use their perfectionism as an excuse and to seek sympathy from others.
- At its worst, this form of perfectionism can cause depression and alienation from colleagues.
- Too much focus on tiny, often irrelevant, details makes these people lose touch and energy and results in low productivity.
- They've got to reach the ideal no matter what. For them the thing has no value if it is not 100 percent perfect and successful.
- There is only one way to do it: the "right way," which really means "my way." And it is devastating when things go wrong.
- These people have a rigid outlook, which doesn't allow for human imperfection. Friction with coworkers is inevitable.
- If they can't meet expectations, they can be very defeatist.
- This is low self-esteem masquerading as perfectionism. They feel like losers and are consumed by a sense of shame, self-recrimination, and guilt.
- They are full of negative emotions, relentless frustration, self-absorption, and doubt in their own abilities.
- Fear may cause them to conceal their mistakes from others.
- They keep people from developing social skills and emotional regulation skills that help them cope with life.
- They worry nonstop about their performance. They are preoccupied and can even choke under pressure.

What it means to a design manager:
This kind of perfectionism can be damaging to team morale. The all-or-nothing mindset causes a massive eleventh-hour scuttle of the work the team has done for days, only to have a new idea to execute at the last minute. The attitude can blow schedules, budgets, and client relationships. Fear-based action reduces creativity because they go toward the known and avoid taking risks that are so necessary for brilliant innovation.

What to do:
Keep communicating and managing to the creative brief. Ask: Is this design meeting agreed-upon goals? Remind them of the goal over and over. Ask if their new iterations and changes make the design better or just different. Help convince them to present it as is, get client feedback, and then refine it in the next phase of work. Be firm with them.

Quality Control and Quality Assurance

Designers are driven to do great work. The pitfalls of perfectionism notwithstanding, collectively, graphic designers seem to want to create powerful and aesthetically pleasing designs that work hard to meet clients' needs and support business goals. It's all about quality. In graphic design, quality refers to the client's, the designers', and even the design industry's expectations.

Lack of quality in design projects causes

▶ Wasted time
▶ Additional revisions
▶ Increased costs
▶ Decreased team morale
▶ Unhappy clients

To ensure quality in their work, designers may wish to employ a quality control (QC) and quality assurance (QA) program.

QC is about the standard operational activities a company uses to control the quality of its product or service. Some things include

• Clear direction and decision making
• Constant supervision by experienced managers
• Reviews of work for accuracy and completeness
• Accurate documentation of recommendations, decisions, and assumptions

The goal of these procedures is to make sure the work is done right the first time. QC is about inspection and review.

QA confirms that the QC program is effective and ensures that the product and services meet the company's requirements for quality. QA

• Enforces QC standards
• Helps the company make continual improvements
• Reduces errors and omissions

QA is about planning and prevention. It is ongoing and keeps the design firm in top form.

Taking Responsibility for Quality
Practically speaking, a design manager is often responsible for QC and QA in the sense of setting up a work flow system and checking for accuracy and completeness of that work. This person can also monitor, review, and report to external and internal stakeholders. However, usually the creative director has the final say on whether the work meets creative quality standards. Often, this is pretty subjective. The more the design can be judged and evaluated on objective criteria, the more likely quality is

achievable. The creative brief becomes not only the road map for schedule and budget but also an essential QC/QA standard.

Clients and QC/QA

Graphic design has informally adapted to QC/QA. When a client's input and guidance are solicited in development of a creative brief, the client is helping to write a QC plan. Then when the client is involved in a series of milestone reviews as the project progresses, they are essentially participating in QA. One of the main reasons graphic design is an iterative process, with client input and feedback solicited at specific points, is to ensure their review so that quality standards are set and met.

Designers can tell their clients this, and frame their design process in QC/QA terms at the start of a project. If this language and management concept is meaningful to the client, speaking in terms of QC/QA can solidify a client's impression of their design consultant as a bona fide businessperson who possesses artistic and business acumen. This can lead to trust. Warning: Not all clients respond to this kind of language. Some think it's silly, or perhaps haven't even heard of the concept.

Crisis or Problem Management

Sometimes, a project runs into unforeseen difficulties that escalate to real problems, even a crisis. The iterative phased design process of working usually means a project can be stopped at certain points before it becomes a disaster. However, trouble can always strike. Here are some steps to take in a crisis situation:

- Acknowledge that there is a problem/crisis.
- Define the crisis. Rate its severity.
- Meet with critical team members. Determine if the design team can solve the problem. If you can, go ahead and fix it.
- If you can't solve the problem internally, alert the client about the problem immediately. Offer any solution(s) the team has formulated. Get client approval to implement it.
- Either way, act on the plan. Determine if there is any impact to time, costs, and quality that the client expects from this project and must be made aware of.
- Once accomplished, announce that the crisis is over and discuss the outcome. Learn from the situation.

Sometimes, a crisis can pull the team together, and even strengthen the bond with the client. It's all about acting quickly, being truthful, communicating efficiently, and solving the problem.

Project Profile in Managing Creatives:

Kama Sutra Company designed by Chase Design Group / Los Angeles, California USA

Kama Sutra Company

Since founding Chase Design Group in 1986, Margo Chase has consistently led a creative team that has produced award-winning work in many areas of design. Recognized worldwide for her skill with custom typography and identity development, Chase is dedicated to creating client success through high-quality, intelligent creative. Her vision provides the fuel for Chase Design Group's growth and achievement. When Kama Sutra first came to Chase in 1989, it had been through a packaging update that had missed the mark. Sales had eroded and the brand was consistently unable to break out of the adult market into more mainstream gift and specialty retail. The original product, launched in 1965, had an authentic look and a loyal following that had been lost. Over the years, Kama Sutra engaged Chase to help regain lost loyalists and find new ones through the development of packaging and marketing materials for new products.

BELOW
The key to repositioning Kama Sutra was to move the brand away from its "aging hippie" roots and adult (sex) market associations to appeal to a more mainstream consumer. Kama Sutra needed to look appealing and credible, but not overtly sexual. The Kama Sutra brand name evokes the romantic exoticism of India, and this was leveraged in the design so that mainstream gift retailers would not feel embarrassed to display the products in their stores. To fulfill on the equity of the brand name, hand-painted tapestries imported from India became the inspiration for the new design direction.

2.3: The Emotional Target
INSPIRING CONFIDENCE AND AUTHENTICITY

The Kama Sutra brand name evokes the romantic exoticism of India, but the 1980 redesign lost the authenticity of the original packaging. Mainstream gift buyers reported feeling embarrassed to display the current packaging in their stores. Another redesign was needed to create a brand that would inspire confidence. Bill and Maryanne needed to feel proud to have Kama Sutra products on their night stand. To leverage the equity of the brand name, hand-painted tapestries imported from India became the inspiration for the new design direction.

BELOW
The redesign started with a core product overhaul that retained the equity of the original bottle and tube shapes. A new logo, combined with a bright green and gold tapestry pattern, gave the brand a rich, authentic feeling. Indian-inspired floral designs and bright colors helped make the products appealing and distinct. In addition, products grouped in new gift tin designs helped Kama Sutra break into gift and mass markets, increased sales exponentially, and positioned the company for further expansion.

BELOW
Kama Sutra does no advertising, so direct mail and in-store marketing materials are key to educating consumers and helping them discover new products. Wholesale product catalogs help retailers understand the brand through consistent copy tone and product descriptions. Product displays and fixtures help retailers display the full line and introduce new products in a brand-consistent manner.

"I don't feel that there are many designers in the world who are really good at understanding strategy and then are able to translate that strategy into design. There are design firms that do well in one or the other, but few can do the magic that happens when the two come together."
—Margo Chase, founder,
   Chase Design Group

Chapter 7
Managing Clients

Building Lasting Client Collaborations

Creating a strong collaborative partnership with clients is critical for graphic designers. Design is, by and large, a commercially driven applied art form that is nearly always commissioned by a client seeking to send a specific message for a specific purpose, often in service to their business. There would be no design project without a client. Even when designers are creating self-promo materials or their own products, they are their own client with set goals and expectations.

Here are the keys to having a successful and lasting client relationship:

▷ Do what you say you're going to do.
▷ Exceed clients' expectations.
▷ Stay in constant communication.
▷ Treat clients as important contributors.
▷ Create design that works to meet their goals.
▷ Deliver on time and on budget.

The more often you do these things, the more you'll build up your clients' trust and respect, which are at the heart of all long-term designer–client relationships. Building that strong connection with a client is often accomplished by fully involving them in the design process.

Working through Problems

The working relationship between designer and client doesn't always run smoothly, however. The main problems clients may have with designers include

• Missed deadlines
• Miscommunication
• Off-target creative
• Noninvolvement of the principles
• Bad chemistry
• Surprises, creative or financial

The main problems designers have with clients include all of the above, plus

• Excessive revisions
• Fear or issues with the design solution
• Delays in client input or approvals
• Payment delays, or worse, nonpayment of invoices

Other problems can arise during the design process—every job is a custom order, after all. As a policy, it's best to resolve any trouble immediately and as thoroughly as possible.

One area of ongoing difficulty that designers experience has to do with gaining clients' approval of challenging design solutions. There is an art to presenting design well, especially in a way that fosters helpful discussion and, ultimately, client acceptance of the design. Practice makes perfect in this regard. The more you do it, the better you get at it. The better you get at it, the more the client trusts you, and the more they trust you, the more likely they are to approve your design solutions.

Six Tips for Getting Client Approval

Getting clients to buy into the design, no matter what stage the project is in, is vital. Designers must figure out how to sell their ideas to their clients. Accomplishing this is partly informing them and partly charming them, with a lot of salesmanship thrown into the mix. Here are some tips on persuasion:

1 Set the tone.
Be on time, dress to impress, and have presentation materials in order. Establish a friendly bond with the client and show them respect and warmth. Set the stage for them to receive the presentation and listen to you in a positive frame of mind.

2 Summarize the background.
Remind the client of previous discussions. Review any research, strategy, or prior thinking for the work. Sum it up again so that the client understands the context of the current presentation. Reinforce that this is not an arbitrary concept, but a design based on the creative brief.

3 Tell them a story.
Explain briefly how this idea works. Take them through the decision-making process for the design. Do it in narrative form. Show how the idea evolved from the client's goals and that it is a logical conclusion, and, therefore, a perfect design solution.

4 Employ relevant buzzwords.
Speak as the client would speak when talking about the design's goals, context, and appropriateness. Refer to the client's language from briefings. If they wanted to "dominate" or "reignite" or "dazzle," tell them that your idea does exactly that.

5 Give them a solutions hook.
Clients love a short, easily repeatable explanation of the design that they can express to their internal team. Make it clearly definable and memorable. Explain the concept as a sound bite that obviously solves their problem. Let this be the take-away they can explain to others.

6 Know when enough is enough.
Make your case. Do it with confidence. Then stop talking and invite feedback. Think before you speak and especially avoid defense mechanisms.

Case Study in Managing Clients:

Primal Screen/Atlanta, Georgia USA

Primal Screen

Primal Screen is a multiplatform design agency that distills a keen knowledge of brand essence and serves it up to every screen—televisions, computers, mobile telephones, PDAs, and lightweight media receivers. The firm is expert in dynamic media and is poised to bring graphic design wherever communication via screen takes us. Doug Grimmett, founding partner and creative director, leads a creative team that combines the best of the design and animation worlds into something new and ever changing. "Think about it—from Google to YouTube, from iPods to Wii, it is designers who create the experience, build the interface, and give it meaning," says Grimmett. "Design has never been as important as it is now."

BELOW
The Primal Screen website sets the tone for a fun, screen-based experience. Showcasing the firm's work through a series of playfully rendered screens, the website takes the viewer through a creative journey. "Primal Screen can do it all: eel animation, CGI, Flash, live-action combinations," says Pat Giles, associate creative director at Saatchi & Saatchi/NYC. "It has attention to detail and design that rivals other world-class animation studios in London, New York, and Los Angeles."

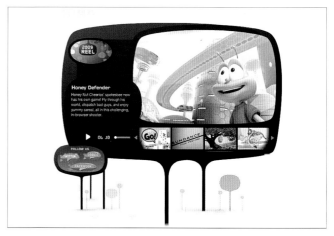

Hallmark Channel: Tell Us Your Story

Hallmark Channel is about stories. To build a strong connection to its core audience, the television network gives viewers an opportunity to phone in amusing or sweet stories from their lives. Stories that are selected are animated and streamed online at the network's "Tell Us Your Story" website, and sometimes aired on TV as well. This story, "Garfield," captures all the discord and harmony of the American holiday, Thanksgiving, in thirty seconds. What's more, it reinforces Hallmark as a family-oriented and holiday-focused brand.

"The one thing I wish every client understood about working with a designer is the incredible power and value of good design. Most clients do not get it, but good clients get it instinctively."
—Doug Grimmett, founding partner and creative director, Primal Screen

Case Study in Managing Clients:

Primal Screen / Atlanta, Georgia USA

PBS KIDS

PBS offers everyone opportunities for exploration and discovery through content on TV, mobile devices, new media, the Web, and community programs. PBS KIDS is an iconic extension of the PBS brand. It is a trusted guide for little explorers, from every walk of life as they discover themselves and the wonder-filled world around them. The main creative challenge was to infuse the presentation of the brand with its explorer archetype. The PBS KIDS logo features two animated preschool characters. Primal Screen developed a world where these characters could explore and experiment in a laboratory for discovery. Visually, cutout paper, felt, pipe cleaners, and other craft materials familiar to preschoolers created opportunities for the brand's preschool audience to explore the everyday world around them.

TCM Prime Time Movie Open

Turner Broadcasting Network's flagship primetime movie event, Turner Classic Movies (TCM), wanted to create an opener that took place in a monumental movie theater. "Of course, no single building could contain all of TCM's film goodness, so we built a citywide cinematheque," explains Grimmett. "The actors are live-action, but the backgrounds are computer-generated graphics to heighten the drama with expressionistic lighting and powerful camera moves. And while the structures may be entirely digital, the scenes are as real as the celluloid we all love so much."

Designers must do the following three things to keep their clients happy:
1. Manage expectations; carefully define the parameters and deliverables.
2. Once expectations are firmly established, exceed them.
3. Listen carefully and send notes with action items after every review.
—Doug Grimmett, founding partner and creative director, Primal Screen

How to Run a Creative Meeting

Throughout the design process, no matter what the project, every graphic designer has to have meetings. Some are internal, and some of the most important ones are with clients. Here are some recommendations regarding meetings.

The main reasons to have a meeting:
- Evaluate information.
- Make decisions.
- Make key creative presentations.
- Inspire the team.
- Bring people together.

Don't call a meeting if you
- Have a simple message to deliver, especially if it requires no immediate answer
- Are more persuasive on paper or via telephone than face to face
- Can reach your goal by other means

If you must call a meeting
- Prepare for it in advance.
- Define the meeting's purpose and goals.
- Invite the minimum number of essential people to attend.
- Create an agenda, send it before the meeting, and stick to it at the meeting.
- Make sure all attendees have the relevant logistical information (location, time, parking, etc.).
- Start and end the meeting on time.
- Keep it short and to the point, but make sure all attendees have a chance for input.
- Present only relevant background information.
- Emphasize people—listen to the group, exchange ideas, stimulate discussion.
- Assign follow-up action items and then make sure they are done.
- Close the meeting by summarizing decisions and next steps.
- Confirm commitments and responsibilities.

A meeting will tend to fail because
- It was unnecessary or held for the wrong reason.
- The objectives and goals weren't clear.
- The wrong people were present.
- It was badly timed.
- It wasn't properly controlled and was subject to poor decision making.
- It took place in an uncomfortable environment.

To be effective in meetings
- Clarify and summarize.
- Listen and question.
- Concentrate and focus.
- Be polite and patient.
- Serve as a role model.
- Encourage participation.
- Don't dominate the discussion.
- Control your emotions.
- Judge content, not delivery.
- Observe verbal and nonverbal cues.
- Tolerate divergent views.
- Act as a mediator.
- Stay impartial until all information is out.
- Be fearless.

Case Study in Managing Clients:

344 Design, LLC / Los Angeles, California USA

Stefan G. Bucher's firm, 344 Design, is founded on the idea that art best serves commerce if it's built on a solid foundation of truth, integrity, and heart. "Because that's when art actually works. Anything less, starves a soul and isn't worth anyone's time or attention," says Bucher. 344 Design specializes in complex solutions for ambitious clients with graphic design as the starting point. Bucher also does writing, illustration, animation, and music.

LA Louver: David Hockney Catalog

344 Design creates many distinctive publications for the international all-star roster of LA Louver Gallery artists. For David Hockney's exhibition, "The East Yorkshire Landscape," Bucher designed a catalog that mirrors the strong horizontal nature of Hockney's paintings. The seventy-four-page, fully illustrated catalog features a foreword by gallery owner Peter Goulds, with text and paintings by Hockney, who is considered to be one of the most influential artists of the twentieth century and is routinely referred to as "Britain's most famous living artist."

BELOW
The subject of Hockney's paintings is the landscape of East Yorkshire, England, which first engaged his imagination as a teenager and has become a recurring primary source of inspiration for his art. The catalog allows viewers to immerse themselves into these lush landscapes, taking away a feeling of being in a timeless space.

David Hockney
The East Yorkshire Landscape

Case Study in Managing Clients:

344 Design, LLC / Los Angeles, California USA

Designing the Hockney catalog was a dream come true for Bucher. "Not only did I get a private event showing of his amazing new landscape paintings at his Los Angeles studio, but I got to meet the man himself when it came time to present comps," he says. "It's not often that you get to meet one of your heroes, and a rare occasion that they exceed your expectations."

Bucher's client decided to delay publication of the catalog until after the artist's opening show. "This gave us the opportunity to document the paintings in LA Louver's beautiful gallery space, which also gives you a better idea of their monumental scale," Bucher explains. "The design of the catalog is quite minimal. When you're working with brilliant ingredients you don't mess them up with fussy spices or a tricky sauce. That said, I could allow myself one little flourish. Since we are dealing with landscapes, all the painting details are anchored by horizontal lines that align with the horizon of each painting."

Hockney's paintings are very big—up to 40 feet (12.2 m) wide—and most are made by fitting many smaller paintings together, a method that allows the canvases to be easily transported back and forth. Plus, Hockney can work on the individual segments in his studio without standing on a ladder, something that works well for this deaf painter who is well over seventy years old. In creating these paintings, Hockney eschews all use of photography, which standardizes color, flattens perspective, and pushes the viewer away from things. As such, in Hockney's paintings, the viewer is brought into the landscape with an immediacy that is filtered through the artist's experience of place, both felt and remembered.

Woldgate Woods, March 30 – April 21 2006
oil on six canvases.
overall: 73 x 146" (185.4 x 370.8 cm)

FOREWORD

In February and March of this year, L.A. Louver presented an exhibition of new works by David Hockney, entitled *The East Yorkshire Landscape*. This extraordinary group of paintings followed on from a show of David's watercolors,[1] presented in the gallery during 2005. At that time, this exhibition represented the high point of David's achievement with the medium with which he had worked exclusively for the preceding three years. Armed with all of the new knowledge he had acquired from having worked so directly on paper with translucent watercolors, David returned to Los Angeles to prepare for that beautiful exhibition, and to paint with oil on canvas. From this visit a series of portraits of friends emerged, which we in turn had an opportunity to experience in the retrospective exhibition of portraits that traveled from Boston, to Los Angeles, and ultimately to London in 2006 – 2007.[2] Of course, as on many occasions during David's career, making portraits has been a way for the artist to return to the canvas. At this time David's ambition was focused on capturing his response to the East Yorkshire landscape as a subject, and in images centered on his feelings for the place, time and memory from this space of his youth.

Fortunately for us in Southern California, Stephanie Barron, the Senior Curator of Modern Art at the Los Angeles County

Museum of Art, visited David Hockney in his Yorkshire studio during the late summer of 2006. Stephanie was amazed by what the artist had already produced: plein air landscape paintings on canvas, made quickly and boldly with big brushes involving a vivid palette, often on multiple canvases, which were taken out in the four-wheel drive vehicle down country lanes, into the open fields. During this visit, Stephanie reminded David that the great touring exhibition of John Constable's studio landscape paintings,[3] together with his controversial attendant six-foot sketches of the same subjects, would soon be traveling to its last venue at the Huntington in San Marino, California. Stephanie suggested to David that an audience should have the opportunity to experience two English painters, concerned in their respective times with innovative ways of considering landscape painting. Soon David was on the phone, and the idea of *The East Yorkshire Landscape* exhibition was born.

Given the spontaneity of this decision and the urgency with which David was pursuing his new motifs, we decided to publish the accompanying exhibition catalogue at a later date. This timing enabled David to utilize every available minute to work with his chosen landscape subject, through the changing seasons, and to be able to respond, in real time, to feelings evoked from the diminishing duration of daylight,

seasonal changing foliage, and nature's definition of space. This decision also meant that we could leave our selection of the paintings to be exhibited to the very last minute available, and for David to plan precisely how these works could be uniquely installed in the gallery. As such, in this catalogue we made a selection of installation photographs to memorialize the experience of the show. A short film[4] was also made for L.A. Louver. This, together with a complete account of the exhibition, can be viewed on our Web site[5].

Five of the paintings entitled *Woldgate Woods* were selected from an ongoing, as yet to be completed series of paintings of the four seasons. Following a visit to the Constable exhibition in San Marino and to David's Los Angeles studio by Stephen Deuchar, Director of Tate Britain, it was decided that this same group of paintings would also be shown at the Tate. From the summer of 2007 until February 2008, these five *Woldgate Woods* paintings can be seen at Tate Britain,[6] to coincide with an exhibition of J.M.W. Turner's watercolors, selected by David Hockney from the museum's significant holdings.[7]

While David Hockney was in Los Angeles for *The East Yorkshire Landscape* exhibition, he began to ponder how far this idea of multiple-canvas "combine" paintings could be

Case Study in Managing Clients:

344 Design, LLC / Los Angeles, California USA

The format of the catalog is 15 × 9 inches (38.1 × 22.8 cm), a size that works well with the oil paintings' format, and is impressive to hold in your hands. All the images are finished with a spot gloss varnish. The inside of the high-gloss dust jacket has a subtle double hit of hot pink ink. "We selected a number of painting details for the catalog divider pages," notes Bucher. "They are reproduced at 100 percent scale. While the paintings are designed to look startlingly realistic and pastoral when viewed at about 80 feet [24.4 m], they reveal themselves to be highly stylized and full of motion at close range." "As part of the process, Mr. Hockney's assistant takes hundreds of photographs of each painting taking shape," says Bucher. "This allows him to review his own project progress from day to day. It also gave me wonderful material for the catalog. How often do you get the chance to show not only the beautiful end result, but also a behind-the-scenes look at its creation?"

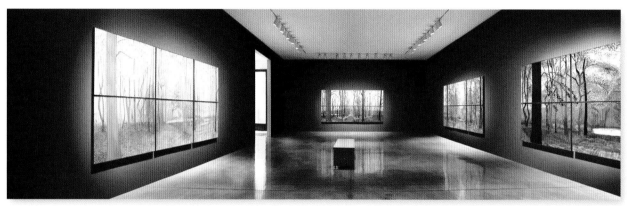

Stefan G. Bucher on Clients

Q. What do you think are the three most essential things a designer must do in order to keep their clients happy?
A. Be useful. Be true to your word. Be a mensch.

I'm always shocked when clients are grateful when I simply do what I said I would when I said I would. To me, that's basic business conduct. Hell, that's basic human conduct. You deliver what you promise. But apparently this puts me ahead of many other designers. In the rare instances, when I can't stick to my promise, I say so as soon as I know it'll happen, so we can minimize the damage. Over the past few years, I've worked with a few vendors that turned out to be often late, often careless, but never at a loss for excuses or a passive aggressive attitude. That's a serious drag, but a great education, because it put this thought firmly into my mind: How can I be most helpful to my clients? How can I make their day better for having dealt with me? What do they need out of this project, both in terms of the end result and their day-to-day process?

There is this idea out there that clients will water everything down, and that we need to fight them to get our aesthetic solutions through, because they don't trust us. Well, a lot of times they actually don't. I think it's because they've been burned in the past. If we want clients to trust us, we have to deliver on the day-to-day stuff by behaving like adults, and by being menschy about it. Manners and follow-through will open any door eventually. As soon as I was able to approach my clients as somebody wanting to help them versus somebody protecting a nascent portfolio piece, they started listening to me. Because they could see that I truly had their best interests at heart. (And that, of course, actually led to much better work for my portfolio.)

Q. How did you learn to effectively work with clients? Was there one huge learning opportunity or an evolving understanding?
A. Working effectively with clients, was and is, an evolving understanding, but there were definitely markers along the way. A big step came with my doing editorial and self-generated work. That let me to get a lot of the things off my mind and on press without having to wedge them into client projects.

The big revelation was trying to hire outside creative help, and becoming a client myself. Some of the people I worked with were great. They addressed my requests, and then exceeded them. Others either fought me constantly or just went sour and limp. I recognized that I had sometimes done that in the past, and that it wasn't doing anybody any good. In fact, it made me into a horrendous micromanager— the kind of awful, nasty client every designer mutters about under his or her breath. The one thing I wanted was to make my life easier by paying somebody else to help me. Instead, I had to sit on people every day to extract a product that I then had to fix, if not redo outright, only to catch attitude for doing so. It forcefully put the idea of being useful at the top of my list.

Realize, please, that I'm not saying just roll over and do whatever the client wants. I'm saying try, as much as you can, to put yourself into the client's shoes to understand what they need. It'll let you ask better questions, which will give you better information, which will let you do better work that's easier for the client to approve. It will also make their life easier, which will make them trust you more, which will give you the confidence to do even better work.

Q. What is the one thing you wish every client understood about how to work with a designer?
A. Some clients don't understand that what we do is art—art applied to a commercial purpose, but art nonetheless. They may think that we treat our job as they treat theirs— as a professional task that's important, but doesn't define them. They may not understand that a bump in type size causes serious mental discomfort. Many do understand, but it's not a priority for them. Nor should it be. When I pay for somebody's help, I try very hard to make sure that they can be proud of the result of their labor, but in the end I need to get a product that's at least as good as what I had in mind. If I'm not getting that I'm going to enforce the changes I feel are necessary. (This is why I work alone and do 99.9% of everything myself.)

Q. What's the one thing you wish every client understood about how to work with a designer?
A. Every copy revision means fixing the rag again. Stop it!

Case Study in Managing Clients:

344 Design, LLC / Los Angeles, California USA

The Graphic Eye

The Graphic Eye is a collection of photographs taken by graphic designers from around the globe. It is highly personal work from some of the world's most innovative graphic designers, including big international names such as Ed Fella, Jeri Heiden, Sean Adams, and Marian Bantjes. The images in *The Graphic Eye* offer a glimpse into the working methods and obsessions of this unique class of visual creatives. Detail-oriented and aesthetically demanding, graphic designers have a special way of looking at the world, and the photographic images they create for their own reference and enjoyment—from micro details to monumental cityscapes, funny vignettes to found fashion—are as unconventional as they are inspirational.

Chris Rubino

Opposite:

Top Three:

Above left:

Alexander Stadler

Above right:

Brandy Flower Robato

Opposite:
Above top left:
Above top right:
Above bottom:

Brandy Flower Robato

Opposite top row, left to right:

Opposite second row, left to right:

Opposite third row, left to right:

Opposite fourth row, left to right:

Above:

Michael Bierut Talks about Clients

Clients can be the best part of the design process.

Clients are the difference between art and design.

My clients are the same as yours.

The right client can change anything.

The best clients love design or don't give a damn about it.
(i.e., they have confidence)

The worst clients are somewhere in between (i.e., they have fear).

Never talk about "educating the client."

What makes a great client? brains, passion, trust—and courage.

"You'll never go wrong when you work with someone smarter than you."
(the late graphic designer, Tibor Kalman)

Warning: Your great client may not be my great client.

Great clients lead to more great clients (and more great work).

Bad clients lead to more bad clients (and more bad work).

Bad clients take up more of your time than they should.

Meanwhile, we take great clients for granted.

The trick is to reverse this.

What do I owe a great client? Loyalty, honesty, dedication, and tenacity.

Once you find a great client, never let them go.

If you can find five great clients, you're set for life.

"You better find somebody to love."
(by Darby Slick, performed by Jefferson Airplane)

Good luck.

Michael Bierut is a partner at the multidisciplinary design firm, Pentagram in New York (www.pentagram.com) and is an editor of the online design magazine, *Design Observer* (www.designobserver.com.) His talk was part of an AIGA New York 2010 Creative Mornings series. Thanks to Paul Soulellis of Soulellis Studio for the speech transcription.

Project Profile in Managing Clients:

Aspen Leaf Soap Factory designed by Dig Design / Milwaukee, Wisconsin USA

Aspen Leaf Soap Factory

Dig Design, led by creative director Amy Decker, believes that "good design is good business." Its work for the Aspen Leaf Soap Factory (ASLF) proves just that. The client had been selling handcrafted olive oil soap at Colorado farmer's markets, where they created a loyal following and were asked by local hotels and resorts to carry their handcrafted natural soaps made from pure essential oils. This stirred their ambitions to grow the brand and eventually open their own retail boutique. Dig Design redesigned the identity and expanded product line packaging while highlighting the handcrafted aspect and Aspen location. The rebranding enhanced visibility and created a strong shelf presence.

The initial focus was to create a packaging system to have the products stand alone on the shelf, yet belong to the overall product family. Five new product segments were introduced, twelve products in all. The target audience was local Aspen residents and tourists to this upscale resort ski town looking for a natural alternative soap for personal use and as gifts that performed better than commercial soap.

"It was important to treat the design of the mark as a refinement of the original, as they had been in business for many years and had a strong local following for their products," says Decker. "After discussing and reviewing the brand, we determined the important elements to keep in the redesign were the leaf pattern and the typeface ITC Cancione. Keeping those would bridge the old with the new successfully."

"All the olive oil soaps were using the same package with stickers indicating the different aromas when we started working together," explains Decker. "That was the cost-effective way for ALSF to package the soaps. When I was hired to redesign the packages, they wanted to continue that practice, and for the first round of packaging we did. However, as they were growing and entering into new stores, as well as readying to open their own store, they agreed to have a product line created with a color-coded system for the aromas they use."

"In the final version," notes Decker, "I chose the copper color for the whole word-mark, and kept the black for 'soap factory.' This allowed us to keep the sage green background colors, and incorporate a soft color palette in the leaf pattern for the product color ways and have the mark pop off the background. I also feel the copper is earthier and speaks to the natural handmade qualities. Using the copper on both the mark and the product name ties them together and balances the labels."

Project Profile in Profitability:

Various Posters designed by AdamsMorioka / Los Angeles, California, and New York, New York USA

AdamsMorioka Posters

Founded in 1994 by creative director Sean Adams and Noreen Morioka, AdamsMorioka Inc. is a multidisciplinary design firm whose work ranges from corporate identities, identity systems, print campaigns, and environmental graphics to motion and digital projects, animation, and websites. Their work has garnered awards and recognition around the world. Some of their most provocative and intriguing work has been for themselves. Over the years, they have created numerous posters to advertise their speaking engagements from Milwaukee, Wisconsin, to Cape Town, South Africa. A series of promotional posters for AdamsMorioka lectures appear below and opposite. Each one gives a new take on the design firm's brand image.

"With our clients, we listen, listen, listen, and make sure we are articulating their vision. Being our own client is sometimes exciting and sometimes scary. I've noticed that when we listen to the voices in our heads, things can get a little bit crazy."
—Sean Adams, creative director, AdamsMorioka

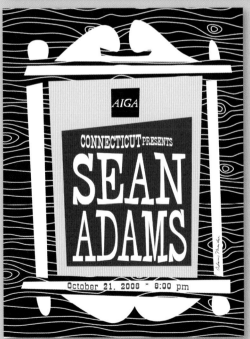

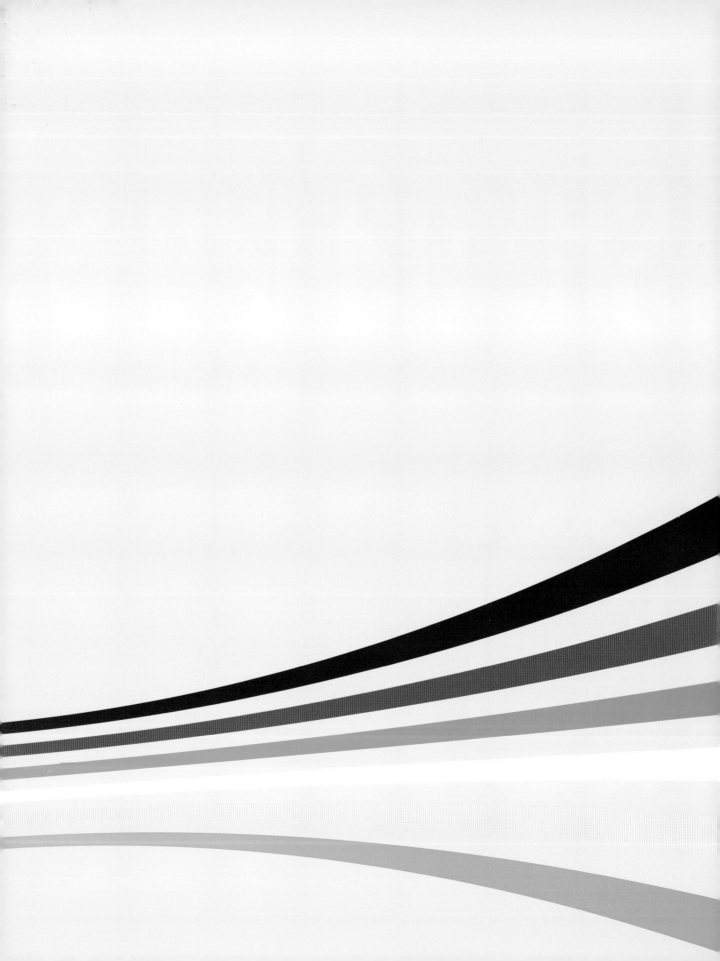

Chapter 8
Profitability

Being Profitable in Graphic Design

Although many people get into graphic design for the joy of creating things, they remain in it because they become at least workably good at all the business aspects of design. They learn to handle projects with quality, ingenuity, and accuracy; develop interesting and fruitful collaborative relationships; and subsequently are compensated fairly for all of these activities. One thing that keeps designers in businesses that are thriving is to understand and monitor the profitability of their client relationships.

Profitability is the income generated from your work minus the expenses incurred to make that income. The difference in those two numbers is called profit, and the measurement ratio of profits is called profitability. In addition to the many creative and client requirements, the goal of every design project should be to manage it with profitability in mind.

There are a few ways to look at profitability that are useful for graphic designers:

- By project: How did you do on a particular assignment?
- By client: Over the course of your working relationship, are you profitable on this client's projects?
- By employee: Does this person deliver great work in less time than estimated? On every client's jobs? What types of projects are best?
- By task: Are you better at and more profitable with logo design or web animation? What activities and services give you the highest return on your time?
- By time: Is there a time of the year when we do business that is at higher earnings?
- Overall: Looking at an entire month (or quarter, or year), are we actually losing or making money?

What Impacts Profitability

Many things impact a designer's profitability. Some can be easily controlled, and others are more difficult to alter. Here are a few factors to consider:

- Your clients: Certain categories of clients pay more. Some industries are not as lucrative as others. For example, a publishing company pays less than a Fortune 100 consumer product corporation. Also, do they make endless revisions? Do you let them?
- Your pricing structure: Are you competitive in the marketplace? Are you charging too little? Are your calculations off?
- Your estimating: Are you pricing accurately? Do you allow enough time? Do you include all fees and expenses you're entitled to?
- Your project management: Are you consistently reviewing, monitoring, and managing team work flow according to your plan? What areas are strong? What are weak?

- Your work: Some forms of graphic design do pay more—for example, animation bills out more than newsletters. Do you make more money with particular delivery media than others?
- Your productivity: Do you work efficiently and make decisions quickly? Are you mindful of budgets?

Do It Better Next Time

Learn from current projects so that you can increase profitability in the future. In addition to the postmortem, look at the following financial reports, which you or your bookkeeper can generate from accounting software and, in some cases, from project management software:

- Actual sales (open jobs) versus forecasts or projected sales (list of proposals): This helps you understand if you are priced properly in the marketplace, among other things.
- Estimates versus actual costs: This lets you know how good your estimating, project management, and productivity are.
- Gross margin versus overhead: This shows if your investment in overhead (people and facilities) is paying off and helping you make money (or not).

Through these hard-core evaluations, designers can get set aside emotional attachments to clients and projects and look at what they do best in terms of financial gain. Money isn't everything, but it does affect a designer's creative output, working relationships, and general enjoyment of his or her work. Loving what you do is important, but you must balance that with making a viable income.

Project Postmortems

The only way to understand what is influencing a design firm's profitability is to review business data carefully. One of the most significant measurements is looking deeply into your work breakdown structure and comparing it to what your time sheets and expense reports reveal what really happened on the job. Some project management software allows for this comparison very easily. Whether you are doing it using software or via some other kind of system, this kind of job postmortem yields a lot of valuable information.

To do a postmortem or exit review, ask yourself

- How well did we meet the client's brief? Is the client satisfied?
- How differently was the project implemented from our planning of it? Why? Why not?
- Were there significant changes to time, scope, and schedule? Did we change-order the client for these revisions?
- How do the estimated fees and expenses compare with actual costs?
- How effective were our quality control and quality assurance efforts? What can we do better next time?
- What were the impediments to creativity and productivity? Can we control any of these things better in the future?
- What was our profit on this project? Can we recoup any loss on a future project with this client?
- Ultimately, what were the lessons learned on this project, from this client relationship?

Eight Things That Help Increase Profitability

1. Be lean and mean.

Cut overhead and extraneous spending. The fastest way to boost your profits is to reduce your costs. Fancy offices may or may not be required by your clients. Think long and hard about this. After salaries, rent is often the highest-ticket item in any firm's budget.

2. Get the right clients.

Some work is for love, some is for money. Some clients allow creative innovation, but have minimal to no budgets. Other clients pay more, but their work is less creatively satisfying. The right combination of clients, project types, and opportunities makes for a great balance creatively and financially. However, some design firms have great success with niche markets—it makes them work more effectively. It also can be easier to market themselves because they become known as experts in a particular field. Some designers would be bored to tears with the strategy, and have to mix it up. Either way, identify your most productive and profitable clients and focus on getting more of those.

3. Seek repeat business.

It is easier and cheaper in terms of self-promotional and proposal writing costs to get more business from an existing client than to cultivate a new one. Plus, there's the added bonus of knowing the client's preferences, processes, and personalities—and doing work to suit those things. But remember, putting all your eggs in one basket and have only a limited number of large clients is a risky business strategy.

4. Adjust pricing.

Increase your hourly rate. Resist discounts or arbitrary price cuts. Have a clear and definitive pricing structure that all of your clients can come to know and understand. Keep everything above board and understandable. If you want to cut the price, make sure you cut the scope of work. It's far better to walk away from a job that can't be priced right for your firm, than to do it on the cheap and think you'll get ahead next time. Wait until the next opportunity comes around and bid again.

5. Improve estimating.

Stay competitive, but make sure you estimate your work in a way you can really make money. Compare estimates on jobs to actual job costs all the time, and watch for trends—learn how your team really works, and do your estimating according to that reality. Compare notes with peers, if possible, or ask clients for feedback.

6. Determine a strategy: volume or value.

A traditional business model is to either strive for a high volume of jobs with low profit margins, or go for a low percentage of jobs or sales but each with a higher profit. Competing on low prices means working extremely efficiently, and that's not always possible with the custom-made nature of graphic design. It's probably better to sell your services as a premium product versus a cost-effective consultancy unless you can deliver on the high-volume concept.

7. Boost productivity.

Do the right job, complying with the creative brief, right away. Avoid time-wasting revisions and errors. Avoid redesigns due to internal miscommunication or indecisiveness. Inform the design team of their hard targets in terms of deadlines and hours of work estimated, and then manage them to it. Make sure your employees have proper training, and are on the right projects doing the right tasks based on each individual's skills.

8. Be accountable.

Keep good records. Make sure everyone records their time accurately and consistently. Review projects creatively and financially, on a regular basis. Involve key players in these reviews, and get their input. Learn and adjust—create a culture of continuous improvement. Be aware of profitability, and create and maintain systems and procedures that support profits as well as creativity.

Case Study in Profitability:

And Partners / New York, New York USA

Acting on his desire to create the core brand itself, David Schimmel founded And Partners in 1999 to provide brand strategy, corporate identity, advertising, websites, graphics for mobile devices, and marketing collateral for up-market consumer and professional-service companies. The firm has enjoyed steady growth and recognition while increasingly expanding into multimedia and environments. "We believe in design," says Schimmel. "Not only in its capacity to make an entity attractive and accessible, but also for its ability to build business, create and differentiate brands, and command a premium."

Neenah Paper Think Ink

And Partners brought an unconventional idea to Neenah Paper this spring: Sell paper by writing software. Schimmel and team co-conceived and designed an iPhone application to coordinate with Neenah's longstanding paper information resource called Think Ink. The extension into the world of mobile applications was natural for Neenah, as it had already developed BlackBerry apps for its business partners. The entry into the world of iPhone apps evolved as a means to peruse color combinations to create unique palettes. This powerful interactive tool includes shade and hue variations and has a built-in sample paper ordering capability.

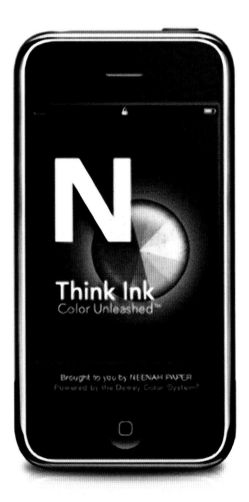

OPPOSITE
Think Ink is a free iPhone application that enables users to identify colors via the Dewey Color System, the world's only scientifically validated color-based personality testing instrument. It empirically predicts the recognized major psychometric personality factors without language—its practical application is a reliable and quick reference tool for the correlated brand attributes of colors.

BELOW
Since inspiration can strike anywhere and at any time, designers now have the freedom to capture their inspiration in real time, via photography using the iPhone, and then select an instantaneous color palette with a full range of paper assortments for a design project or idea.

"More than anything, it's always been about people. It's not necessarily the best designers who have all of the opportunities. Sometimes, it's about personality and temperament. People work with who they want to work with—not always who is best for a particular job. It's wonderful because it fosters a level of loyalty from clients and makes it rewarding because when they appreciate what you do, they come back to you again and again."

—David Schimmel, creative director, And Partners

Case Study in Profitability:

And Partners / New York, New York USA

THIS PAGE AND OPPOSITE
"We wanted to give designers and printers the ability to pull inspiration from a variety of resources—be it a vibrant green on a blade of grass or a pale shade of butter yellow—to create perfect color palettes for their projects," says Tom Wright, senior director of advertising and design for Neenah Paper. "This application is unlike anything on the market. Users can translate the source of their inspiration into an immediate color palette and select a paper that best enhances their design."

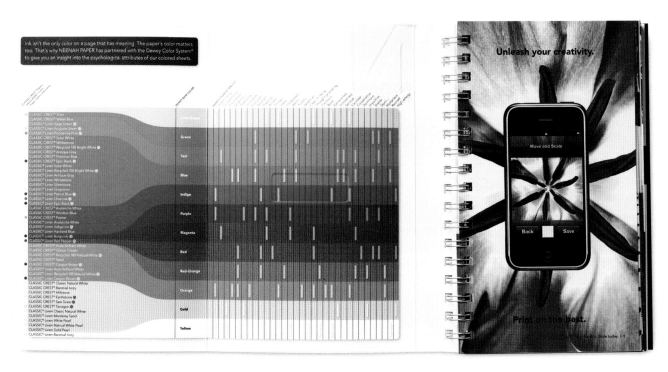

Design Project P&Ls

Profit and Loss Statements, also known as P&Ls, are a standard financial document that shows a business's economic health—or lack thereof. The document summarizes revenue and expenses for a specific period of time, such as a quarter of the year (three months) or the entire year. When looked at for the entire company finances, a P&L may also be referred to as an Income Statement or Earnings Statement. It's a good idea for a design firm to have their bookkeeper create one of these documents so that the state of the firm's finances can be assessed.

It's also a very good idea to have the project manager pull a similar report on projects as they are completed. This allows a project post-mortem to include not just a review of the overall design, and a look back at the client–designer relationship, but also a clear financial analysis as well. These kinds of reviews help designers to understand what profitability is for them and how best to achieve it on a project-by-project basis.

Here's a basic formula to follow to create a project P&L:

1. Look at Fees (Estimates versus Actuals):

Estimated Fee

— Actual Labor (employee's hourly rate × total number of hours)

= *Profit on Labor*

Change Order(s) Fee (if applicable)

— Actual Labor (employee's hourly rate × total number of hours)

= *Profit on Change Ordered Labor*

2. Look at Expenses:

Actual Expenses = _____

Markup on Expenses = _____ (= Profit on Expenses)

3. Total It Up:

Total Profit on Labor

Profit on Change Ordered Labor

+ Profit on Expenses

= *Profit on Job*

Just reviewing these figures on a continual basis keeps managers on top of the financial picture. These P&Ls also begin to create an outline of client relationships, employee productivity, and estimating acumen, as well, by revealing discrepancies between what was anticipated and what actually occurred.

The Importance of Ongoing Design Management

Design management is challenging. Running a graphic design business is, for the most part, exceptionally challenging. Being successful at a service-oriented consulting profession such as graphic design is difficult to accomplish consistently year after year, all while maintaining creative excellence.

Just as designers constantly strive to improve their creative and technical skills, they also need to work on growing their communication and business skills. This is the ongoing practice of design management that has been the subject of this book. And it is the essence of building great client relationships. Finding and attracting those great client relationships is an ongoing game worth engaging in.

Profit from Good Relationships

Clients have difficulty sometimes understanding the difference between one designer and another. They review their portfolios, ask a few questions about their process, but rarely get at some of the key issues that will determine whether the designer–client relationship will be effective and enjoyable. Yes, many designers can make great work for their clients, but the central question a client should be asking is: Can this designer make great work for us?

By the same token, a designer should be looking long and hard at a prospective client and asking: Can we really work for this client? Will we be happy? Will they let us do great work? Will we be paid fairly? Are we going to make or lose money on this client? The answers will change day to day.

Profitability is just one indicator to a design firm that it is on the right track and is successful in its practice. There are many other indicators, but at the end of the day, designers can't stay in business if they can't run their practice in a profitable manner and do excellent creative. A designer can't make great work in a chaotic, unprofitable context. It's all about order, insight, and design management.

Project Profile in Profitability:
LUST / The Hague, Netherlands

Thomas Castro, Dimitri Nieuwenhuizen, and Jeroen Barendse are the principals of the Dutch design firm, LUST. Coincidence, process, context, and essence characterize the working methods of LUST. Information design and manipulation plays an important role in all of their projects, whether they are creating books, websites, interactive screens, exhibitions, environmental graphics, art performances, or guerilla marketing and advertising campaigns. The Walker Art Museum in Minneapolis writes, "The trio likens their activity to the moment when you realize that the last piece of a jigsaw puzzle is missing. To them, this sense of incompleteness and indeterminacy is 'a thousand times more interesting than the moment when the puzzle is finished because when that happens, there is nothing more.'"

At Random: Iris

At Random is an ongoing series of unconventional lectures, screenings, debates, workshops, and performances, each with its own character. Artists, designers, scientists and other guest speakers are encouraged to address topics associated with the corresponding exhibition, This edition, created by LUST, was tied to the exhibition At Random? Netwerken en kruisbestuivingen (Networks and Cross-Pollinations), which is an investigation into the creative processes within our present-day networking society.

Project Profile in Profitability:

LUST / The Hague, Netherlands

LUST has developed a design methodology that has been described as process-based or generative-systems-based design. This entails developing an analytical process, which leads eventually to an end product that designs itself. Moreover, LUST is deeply interested in exploring new pathways for design at the cutting edge where new media and information technologies, architecture and urban systems, and graphic design overlap.

The piece that LUST calls *Iris* was a site-specific project for Museum de Paviloens in Almere, Holland. The concept of randomness is shown via a print-on-demand installation. The name Iris comes from the Dutch word for a printing technique referred to as split fountain printing, whereby two inks are mixed directly onto one roll on a printing machine during the printing process. This causes the inks to gradually flow together, creating a smooth gradient from one color to the other on the paper.

"We selected a spectrum of colors to represent the timeline of the six-month exhibit," explains Castro. "The idea was to print, ahead of time, all the collateral needed for the show, including posters, invitations, and catalogs. This resulted in 80,000 A3-size papers stacked in eight columns in the space." Included in the exhibition space was a Docutech printer capable of printing and saddle-stitched binding. This laser printer produced all the print work of the show. The idea was to feed the printer from the colored stacks.

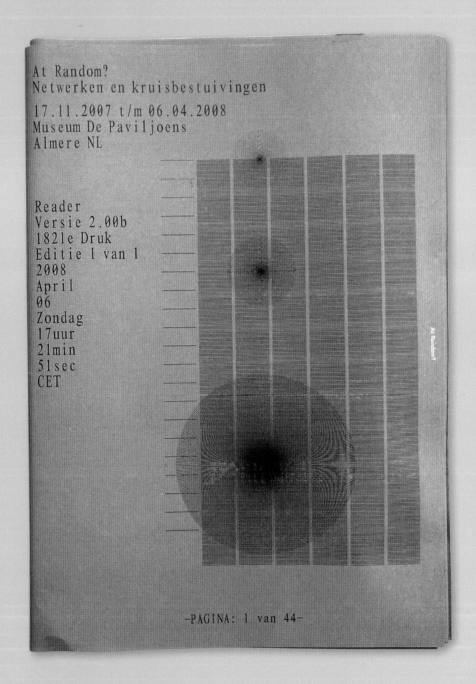

KKEP
Selene Kolman (1966)
Stef Kolman (1967)
Foto's: Martine Stig. (1972)
bliin.com, 2007

In samenwerking met:
Joes Koppers: Front end Design

omschreven als: "a GPS-enhanced real-time

...] and location-based social netwerk. Users can spot and trace each other and share experiences: photo, videos, sound and text in real-time and space on Google Maps. [...] bliin koppelt mensen aan elkaar via hun GPS-locatie. Deze technologie was enkele jaren geleden nog voorbehouden aan automobilisten. Binnen afzienbare tijd zullen steeds meer mobiele telefoons uitgerust met een GPS-ontvanger zijn (Global Positioning System). Speciaal voor deze tentoonstelling zijn de deelnemende kunstenaars en curatoren uitgerust met een GPS-ontvanger op hun mobiele telefoon. Ze zijn ingelogd op de site en kunnen zichzelf en andere deelnemers lokaliseren op de plattegrond van Google Maps en gegevens uitwisselen en tekst, beeld of geluid uploaden. Zodra je bent ingelogd en GPS aanzet, kun de hele wereld zien waar je bent en wat je doet. Want als je met je telefoon een foto maakt en die naar je profiel stuurt, dan verschijnt die foto bij het vijltje op de kaart. Ook je verplaatsingen en de snelheid waarmee je je van A naar B begeeft zijn zichtbaar op bliin. Een van de 400? deelnemers is

fotograaf Martine Stig [...] (1972). De door haar gemaakte clips voor bliin zijn behalve op de website ook in projectie te zien op de

Bronnen in dit examplaar

Marinetti, Filippo Tommaso, Manifesto of Futurism, 1909
www.tag004.nl
www.kweekly.nl, René Passet
Graphic Design in the white cube, www.peterb.sk
nl.wikipedia.org
Koninklijke Bibliotheek
www.rhizome.au, website van Monique Scheepers
Museum De Paviljoens
nl.wikipedia.org

Colofon

Project Profile in Profitability:
LUST / The Hague, Netherlands

The printer was connected to a database of all the catalog text, including the images of the artists' works and the descriptions. Also included were essays and the curator's texts. The exhibition's images were tagged by certain keywords, and each time the button on the printer was pressed it produced a sixty-four-page bound booklet that served as the exhibition catalog. Each time a booklet was printed, the database would decide which image to use with certain words also making each catalog unique.

LUST's ad hoc solution mixes high and low technologies with high concept to maximum effect, as seen in this Title wall for the exhibition.

A timeline was created by the color of the invitation or catalog. As the show went on, the paper dwindled.

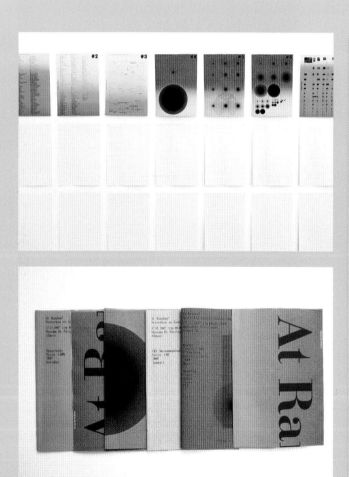

Descriptions of the works were posted to a wall that tracked the data that was printed. This represented the exhibition's network. Each week, new text and new image information updates were made to the network database, which then randomly added this new material to the print material for the show.

For the exhibition posters, LUST used circles to represent the time printed in hours, minutes, and seconds the show was on exhibit. Because of the low resolution of the Docutech printer, the moiré patterns created added another random factor to the piece.

"Today, questions from clients to designers are not always clear. In the design, form and content are no longer strictly separated areas, and there is a continuous interaction between client, designer, and user."
—Thomas Castro, designer, LUST

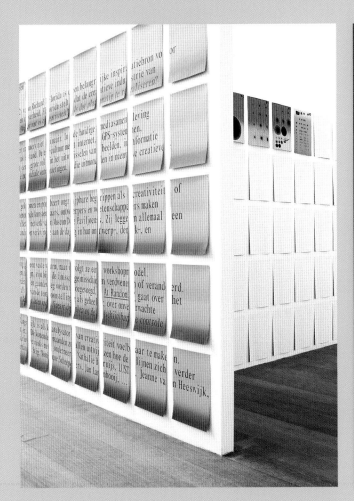

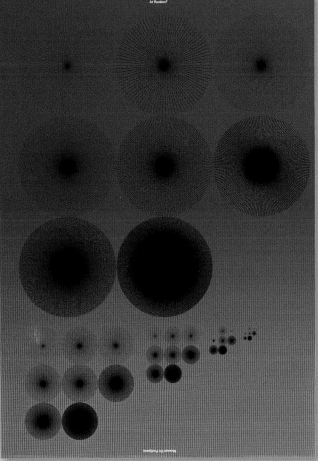

Directory of Contributors

AdamsMorioka
Page: 182
Beverly Hills, CA / New York, NY USA
www.adamsmorioka.com

Collins:
Pages: 34, 37, 38
New York, NY USA
www.collins1.com

Guilherme Marcondes
Page: 156
New York, NY/São Paulo, Brazil
www.guilherme.tv

And Partners
Pages: 190, 192
New York, NY USA
www.andpartnersny.com

Dig Design
Page: 181
Milwaukee, WI USA
www.digdesignmedia.com

Haus Design Communications
Pages: 70, 72, 74
Los Angeles, CA USA
www.madeinhaus.com

Asylum Creative Pte Ltd
Page: 18
Singapore
www.theasylum.com.sg

Fibonacci Design Group
Page: 108
Los Angeles, CA USA
www.fibonaccidesigngroup.com

Larsen
Page: 98
Minneapolis, MN/San Francisco, CA USA
www.larsen.com

Atelier Works
Pages: 54, 56, 57
London, UK
www.atelierworks.co.uk

Finn Creative
Page: 132
Kununurra, Australia
www.finncreative.com.au/

Lorenc + Yoo Design
Pages: 80, 82, 84
Roswell, GA USA
www.lorencyoodesign.com

Chase Design Group
Page: 162
Los Angeles, CA USA
www.chasedesigngroup.com

Good Design Company
Page: 62
Tokyo, Japan
www.gooddesigncompany.com

LUST
Pages: 195, 196
The Hague, Netherlands
www.lust.nl

Martha Rich
Page: 76
Philadelphia, PA USA
www.martharich.com

smashLAB Inc.
Page: 26
Vancouver, BC, Canada
www.smashlab.com/

Umbrella Design
Pages: 140, 142, 144
Mumbai, India
www.umbrelladesign.in

Paprika
Page: 22
Montreal, Canada
www.paparika.com

Sonnenzimmer
Page: 117
Chicago, IL USA
http://sonnenzimmer.com

Voice
Pages: 42, 44, 46
Adelaide, Australia
www.voicedesign.net

Primal Screen
Pages: 168, 170, 171
Atlanta, GA USA
www.primalscreen.com

Sterling Brands
Pages: 148, 150, 152
New York, NY/San Francisco, CA USA
www.sterlingbrands.com

Wallace Church, Inc.
Pages: 120, 122, 124
New York, NY USA
www.wallacechurch.com

Siedemzero
(PawelPiotrPrzybyl)
Page: 88
Warsaw, Poland
www.siedemzero.com

344 Design, LLC
Pages: 173, 174, 176, 178
Los Angeles, CA USA
www.344design.com

Weiden + Kennedy Tokyo
Page: 110
Tokyo, Japan
www.wk.com

Index

Bibliography

For Further Reading (books)

The Business Side of Creativity: The Complete Guide to Running a Small Graphics Design or Communications Business
By Cameron S. Foote and Mark Bellrose, W.W. Norton & Company, Inc., New York, New York, (2006).

The Creative Business Guide to Running a Graphic Design Business
By Cameron S. Foote, W.W. Norton & Company, Inc., New York, New York, (2009).

Graphic Artists Guild Handbook: Pricing & Ethical Guidelines
By The Graphic Artists Guild, North Light Books, Cincinnati, Ohio, (2007).

AIGA Professional Practices in Graphic Design
Second Edition by Tad Crawford, Allworth Press, New York, New York, (2008).

Business and Legal Forms for Graphic Designers
By Tad Crawford and Eva Doman Bruck, Allworth Press, New York, New York, (2003).

Inside The Business of Graphic Design: 60 Leaders Share Their Secrets of Success
By Catharine M. Fischel, Allworth Press, New York, New York, (2003).

Talent Is Not Enough: Business Secrets for Designers
By Shel Perkins, New Riders, Berkeley, California, (2006).

The Business of Graphic Design: A Professional's Handbook
By The Association of Registered Graphic Designers of Ontario (RGD Ontario), RGD Ontario.

How to Be a Graphic Designer without Loosing Your Soul
By Adrian Shaughnessy, Princeton Architectural Press, New York, New York, (2005).

The Business of Graphic Design
By Ed Gold, Watson-Guptill Publications, New York, New York, (1995).

Small Business Kit for Dummies
By Richard D. Harroch, Hungry Minds, New York, New York, (2000).

Whoops! I'm In Business: A Crash Course In Business Basics
By Richard Stim and Lisa Guerin, NOLO, Berkeley, California, (2008).

Keeping the Books: Basic Record Keeping and Accounting for the Successful Small Business
By Linda Pinson Dearborn Trade Publishing, Chicago, Illinois, (2004).

A Guide to the Project Managers Body of Knowledge (PMBOK® Guide) Third Edition
By The Project Management Institute, Newtown Square, Pennsylvania, (2004).

For Further Reading (articles, publications, downloads)

AIGA Standard Form of Agreement For Design Services (PDF pamphlet)
www.aiga.org/content.cfm/standard-agreement

GAIN: AIGA Journal of Business and Design (Online magazine)
www.aiga.org/content.cfm/gain

AIGA Design Business and Ethics (series of PDF pamphlets)
www.aiga.org/content.cfm/design-business-and-ethics

Design Council Business Guides for Designers
www.designcouncil.org.uk/About-Design/Business-Essentials/Business-guides-for-designers/

The Design Management Institute (DMI) Design Management Journal (subscription magazine)

Resources

Design Organizations

AIGA (American Institute of Graphic Arts)
www.aiga.org

AIGA Center for Practice Management
http://cpm.aiga.org/

Association of Product Management and Product Marketing (AIPMM)
www.aipmm.com

Association of Professional Design Firms (APDF)
www.apdf.org

The Association of Registered Graphic Designers of Ontario (RGD Ontario)
www.rgdontario.org

D&AD
www.dandad.org

Danish Design Council
www.ddc.dk

Design Can Change
www.designcanchange.org

Design Council UK
www.designcouncil.org.uk

Design Institute of Australia
www.dia.org.au

Design Management Institute
www.dmi.org

Design Research Society
www.designresearchsociety.org

JAGDA (Japanese Graphic Design Association)
www.jagda.org

Acknowledgments

About the Author

Thank you to the many contributors who added their amazing work and insights to this book. Much of what is covered in this book was learned by trial and error over the many years of my career. Thanks so much to all the designers who I have worked for, especially: Kim Foster, Harry Bua, Alan Urban, Katharina Drexel, Linda Martin, and William Armenteros, Barbara Cohen, Margo Chase, Tim Meraz, Joel Fuller, Monika Zych, Sean Adams, and Noreen Morioka. Many thanks to all of my students at CalArts, Art Center and Otis College of Art and Design who listened patiently as I figured out how to talk about this material in an accessible way. There isn't an audience on earth like art students for showing you in no uncertain terms how to teach something. Seriously. Thanks much to Emily Potts, Betsy Gammons, David Martinell, Cora Hawks, and the entire Rockport team. Much gratitude, as always, to the very talented folks at AdamsMorioka: Sean Adams, Noreen Morioka, Monica Schlaug, Chris Taillon, and Nichelle Narcisi for the great book design. And many thanks to Victor Bornia for everything (and more).

Thank you one and all.

Terry Lee Stone is a design management consultant and writer based in Los Angeles. She has worked with AdamsMorioka, The Designory, and Margo Chase Design among others. Her clients have included: BMW Group DesignworksUSA, Adobe Systems, American Express, USC, and the Sundance Film Festival. Stone has taught the business of design at CalArts, Art Center College of Design, and Otis College of Art and Design. She is co-author of *The Logo Design Workbook*, (Rockport, 2006), and the author of *The Color Design Workbook*, (Rockport, 2008), a second AdamsMorioka book. She has written for several design magazines including *STEP* magazine, *Dynamic Graphics Magazine*, and *AIGA Voice*. Terry served on the board of directors of the AIGA in Atlanta, Los Angeles, and Miami, where she was also the chapter's president. She has presented lectures and workshops for numerous organizations, such as AIGA and the Art Directors Club of New York.